New Da

GW00402488

Edited by **Sally Welch**   September–December 2020

The Bible Reading Fellowship
15 The Chambers, Vineyard
Abingdon OX14 3FE
brf.org.uk

The Bible Reading Fellowship (BRF) is a Registered Charity (233280)

ISBN 978 0 85746 905 2
All rights reserved

This edition © The Bible Reading Fellowship 2020
Cover image © Thinkstock/ stevanovicigor; illustration on page 141 © iStock.com/dddb

Distributed in Australia by:
MediaCom Education Inc, PO Box 610, Unley, SA 5061
Tel: 1 800 811 311 | admin@mediacom.org.au

Distributed in New Zealand by:
Scripture Union Wholesale, PO Box 760, Wellington
Tel: 04 385 0421 | suwholesale@clear.net.nz

Acknowledgements
Scripture quotations marked with the following acronyms are taken from the
version shown. Where no acronym is given, the quotation is taken from the same
version as the headline reference. NIV: The Holy Bible, New International Version,
Anglicised edition, copyright © 1979, 1984, 2011 by Biblica. Used by permission of
Hodder & Stoughton Publishers, an Hachette UK company. All rights reserved. 'NIV'
is a registered trademark of Biblica. UK trademark number 1448790. NRSV: The New
Revised Standard Version of the Bible, Anglicised Edition, copyright © 1989, 1995 by
the Division of Christian Education of the National Council of the Churches of Christ in
the USA. Used by permission. All rights reserved. KJV: Authorised Version of the Bible
(The King James Bible), the rights in which are vested in the Crown; reproduced by
permission of the Crown's Patentee, Cambridge University Press. NLT: The Holy Bible,
New Living Translation, copyright © 1996, 2004, 2015 by Tyndale House Foundation.
Used by permission of Tyndale House Publishers, Inc., Carol Stream, Illinois 60188.
All rights reserved. CEV: Contemporary English Version Copyright © 1991, 1992, 1995
by American Bible Society, Used by Permission. MSG: *The Message*, copyright © 1993,
1994, 1995, 1996, 2000, 2001, 2002 by Eugene H. Peterson. Used by permission of
NavPress. All rights reserved. Represented by Tyndale House Publishers, Inc.

A catalogue record for this book is available from the British Library

Printed by Gutenberg Press, Tarxien, Malta

Suggestions for using *New Daylight*

Find a regular time and place, if possible, where you can read and pray undisturbed. Before you begin, take time to be still and perhaps use the BRF Prayer on page 6. Then read the Bible passage slowly (try reading it aloud if you find it over-familiar), followed by the comment. You can also use *New Daylight* for group study and discussion, if you prefer.

The prayer or point for reflection can be a starting point for your own meditation and prayer. Many people like to keep a journal to record their thoughts about a Bible passage and items for prayer. In *New Daylight* we also note the Sundays and some special festivals from the church calendar, to keep in step with the Christian year.

New Daylight and the Bible

New Daylight contributors use a range of Bible versions, and you will find a list of the versions used opposite. You are welcome to use your own preferred version alongside the passage printed in the notes. This can be particularly helpful if the Bible text has been abridged.

New Daylight affirms that the whole of the Bible is God's revelation to us, and we should read, reflect on and learn from every part of both Old and New Testaments. Usually the printed comment presents a straightforward 'thought for the day', but sometimes it may also raise questions rather than simply providing answers, as we wrestle with some of the more difficult passages of scripture.

New Daylight is also available in a deluxe edition (larger format). Visit your local Christian bookshop or BRF's online shop **brfonline.org.uk**. To obtain a cassette version for the visually impaired, contact Torch Trust for the Blind, Torch House, Torch Way, Northampton Road, Market Harborough LE16 9HL; +44 (0)1858 438260; **info@torchtrust.org**. For a Braille edition, contact St John's Guild, Sovereign House, 12–14 Warwick Street, Coventry CV5 6ET; +44 (0)24 7671 4241; **info@stjohnsguild.org**.

Comment on *New Daylight*

To send feedback, please email **enquiries@brf.org.uk**, phone **+44 (0)1865 319700** or write to the address shown opposite.

Writers in this issue

Denis Alexander, **Ruth Bancewicz**, **Keith Fox**, **Rodney Holder**, **Hugh Rollinson** and **Bob White** all work with the Faraday Institute for Science and Religion. **Jennifer Brown** is tutor for the Cuddesdon School of Theology and Ministry at Ripon College Cuddesdon. **Dave Gregory** is coordinator of Messy Church Does Science. **Cherryl Hunt** is academic registrar for South West Ministry Training Course. **Wilson Poon** is professor of natural philosophy in Edinburgh University. **Meric Srokosz** is professor of physical oceanography at the National Oceanography Centre, Southampton. **Gillian Straine** is a physicist and Anglican priest.

Amanda Bloor is priest-in-charge of Holy Trinity Bembridge, on the Isle of Wight, and assistant director of ordinands for the Diocese of Portsmouth. She enjoys chaplaincy responsibilities with the Army Cadet Force, the RNLI and local sailing clubs.

David Cole is an international spiritual teacher and retreat leader, an award-winning author and the deputy guardian for the Community of Aidan and Hilda. His BRF books include *Celtic Lent*, *Celtic Advent* and *Celtic Saints*.

Tony Horsfall is a freelance trainer and retreat leader based in Yorkshire. He is an elder in his local church and the author of several books, including *Mentoring Conversations* (BRF, 2020).

Geoffrey Lowson is a retired priest living in the west of County Durham. He spent 21 years working for the mission agency USPG.

Michael Mitton is an Anglican priest, a writer, a speaker and a spiritual director. He has written several books for BRF, including *Travellers of the Heart*, *Seasoned by Seasons* and *Restoring the Woven Cord*.

Stephen Rand worked with Tearfund and Open Doors and, while now retired, he is still the web editor for the All Party Parliamentary Group for International Freedom of Religion or Belief.

Elizabeth Rundle is a retired Methodist minister and author of many study and devotional books and scripts for local and national radio and television.

Veronica Zundel is an Oxford graduate, a writer and a columnist. She is the author of *Everything I Know about God, I've Learned from Being a Parent* (BRF, 2013).

Sally Welch writes…

As I look out of the window of my study, I can see a beautiful copper beech in its full, glorious, multihued splendour. It stands proud and tall, shading the vicarage garden with its thick, glossy leaves. This morning as I admired it, however, I felt overwhelmingly sad, for I knew that it would be only a short time before its leaves began to fall in great drifts on our lawn, and another winter would be upon us. For children and young adults in the northern hemisphere, autumn leaves signify new beginnings as schools, classes and meetings begin once again. As we get older, however, the danger is that we will feel only apprehension at the prospect of winter's challenges of sunless days and cold nights. We must strive against this – the latest research demonstrates that optimists live longer, as well as bringing more joy to those around them. Bare-leaved trees reveal the rolling hills and fields of the Cotswold landscape where I live; past occupations make way for new ones. The love of God still surrounds us; our gifts and experience are still valuable to our communities; our prayerful wisdom grounds ambitious plans and projects.

Rather than bewailing the death of summer, Ruth Bancewicz and her team of scientists help us to see God at work in creation in a new way, as they share Christian approaches to creation. Amanda Bloor's imaginative exploration of ways of praying with everyday objects will help us stretch our 'prayer muscles' as she offers us new ways of encountering God, as part of our contribution to BRF's Holy Habits initiative. Geoffrey Lowson encourages us to lift the 'shroud of mystery' cloaking Deuteronomy and glimpse the coming of the kingdom in its verses. And, in the run-up to Christmas, Veronica Zundel will take us through that wonderful tradition of the Nine Lessons and Carols, beloved by so many, as we encounter once more the beauty of the story of Christ's nativity, which holds the seeds of our redemption.

So let us look forward to the next four months in prayerful anticipation of the signs of God's providence which surround all of us, eager to explore new landscapes opening before us, knowing that we are cradled, now as always, in the hollow of his hand.

The BRF Prayer

Almighty God,
you have taught us that your word is a lamp for our feet
and a light for our path. Help us, and all who prayerfully
read your word, to deepen our fellowship with you
and with each other through your love.
And in so doing may we come to know you more fully,
love you more truly and follow more faithfully
in the steps of your Son Jesus Christ, who lives and reigns
with you and the Holy Spirit, one God forevermore.
Amen

Were you there? BRF celebrates its centenary in 2022 and we'd love you to share your BRF memories with us. We've already heard from supporters with wonderful stories. Beryl Fudge attended our 25th anniversary service in Westminster Central Hall in 1947, in the presence of the Queen Mother and Princess Margaret. Catharine Heron was prepared for confirmation in 1945 by our founder, Canon Leslie Mannering, and still has his duplicated notes in their original brown cardboard folder.

Do you have a BRF story to tell, whether of events, people, books or Bible reading notes? Please email **eley.mcainsh@brf.org.uk**, call **01865 319708** or write to **Eley McAinsh** at BRF, 15 The Chambers, Vineyard, Abingdon, OX14 3FE, United Kingdom.

Our creator God

 Not many of us are scientists, but we can all enjoy the excitement of learning something new about the world. You might have been fascinated over the summer by something you saw on holiday, a new bird appearing in your garden or a nature documentary. Each of us will find that different things provoke our curiosity, prompting us to think of those questions adults often forget to ask: 'What is it?', 'What's it for?' and 'Why?'

The first of September is the beginning of the Season of Creation in the liturgical year, and it is worth stopping to think about what that means today. We understand far more about the mechanisms of how things came to be than the biblical writers could have imagined. We know about the Big Bang, and how living things developed and became more complex over time. We can appreciate the huge diversity and interconnectedness of life on earth. When we learn more about the world, it widens our perspective, giving us a bigger picture of creation and the creator. That informed perspective can help us praise God all the more: what a wonderful world he made!

This series is written by twelve different scientists who are also people of faith. Drawing on a variety of creation passages throughout the Old and New Testaments, we will share just a few of the wonders revealed by science, showing how this perspective expands and enhances our own view of God as creator. I hope you enjoy the new slant that a little bit of science can give to passages which will be familiar friends to many of our readers. Let's enjoy exploring God's good world.

RUTH BANCEWICZ, REFLECTIONS EDITOR

Christt the creator

In these last days he has spoken to us by his Son, whom he appointed heir of all things, and through whom also he made the universe. The Son is the radiance of God's glory and the exact representation of his being, sustaining all things by his powerful word. After he had provided purification for sins, he sat down at the right hand of the Majesty in heaven.

We now know that the universe contains billions of galaxies, each of which contains billions of stars. The numbers are overwhelming. Today's passage tells us that Christ made them all – the entire universe is his; he made it, and it belongs to him. There are also billions of species of plants, animals and insects on earth. Again, Christ made them all – every part of the universe belongs to him. 'Without him nothing was made that has been made' (John 1:3).

Not only did he create the universe, but he also keeps it all going, sustaining everything for every moment of every day, and he has been doing so ever since the beginning of time. Jesus, the second person of the Trinity, didn't inherit the universe; he made it, and he, the maker, is the same Christ who chose to die to redeem us from our sins.

All this shows God's glory. We see the radiance of his character in the overwhelming greatness of the universe: his concern for every detail, even the parts that human eyes will never see. God spoke the universe into being (Genesis 1), and God's same powerful word sustains every part of the universe. He could write off his creation, but in his love he chooses to sustain it moment by moment, showing his gracious love, power and authority.

The one who spoke the world into being and sustains it day-to-day is the same one who speaks to us. He also created us and saved us. So we can trust him to sustain us, just as he takes care of the rest of his creation.

Thank you, God, that you have created this wonderful world that shows your immense power and authority. Thank you that I can trust you to care for me.

KEITH FOX

Constantly creative

His wisdom is profound, his power is vast. Who has resisted him and come out unscathed? He moves mountains without their knowing it and overturns them in his anger. He shakes the earth from its place and makes its pillars tremble. He speaks to the sun and it does not shine; he seals off the light of the stars. He alone stretches out the heavens and treads on the waves of the sea. He is the Maker of the Bear and Orion, the Pleiades and the constellations of the south. He performs wonders that cannot be fathomed, miracles that cannot be counted.

We have all stared at the sky on a clear night and been awed by the sheer number and beauty of the great array of stars above us. But we can be equally awe-inspired as we look at the very small – these days with the help of fancy microscopes. Our own bodies contain around ten trillion cells, of which around 100 billion are brain cells. And if you add up all the connections between those brain cells, that comes to something like 500 trillion. Our own brains are the most complex known structures in the universe. And like the stars, which die and are being formed every day, only numerically far more so, around 240 billion cells are being replaced in our bodies every day.

So just as Job writes, our creator God is an incredibly active creator. Job's insights are all in the present tense: God moves, shakes, speaks, stretches, makes and performs. God is no distant creator who gave the universe some laws back at the beginning to make things work properly, but then withdrew from the action like some absentee landlord. No, God is the one who is constantly creating and upholding everything that exists.

God's wisdom is profound and he performs wonders that cannot be fathomed. Science is simply an attempt to describe and understand those wonders – but really we are only just beginning. Scientists do what Job was doing, describing the works of the constantly creating God, but using a more specialised language. Science can be an important aspect of daily Christian worship.

Lord, give us a fresh vision of your moment-by-moment upholding of your awe-inspiring creation.

DENIS ALEXANDER

God the provider

How many are your works, Lord! In wisdom you made them all; the earth is full of your creatures. There is the sea, vast and spacious, teeming with creatures beyond number – living things both large and small. There the ships go to and fro, and Leviathan, which you formed to frolic there. All creatures look to you to give them their food at the proper time. When you give it to them, they gather it up; when you open your hand, they are satisfied with good things. When you hide your face, they are terrified; when you take away their breath, they die and return to the dust. When you send your Spirit, they are created, and you renew the face of the ground.

One privilege of being an oceanographer, going 'to and fro' on the sea, is experiencing the grandeur of God's creation. On a research trip in the Atlantic we once encountered a Force 11 storm with 12-metre (40-foot) waves, evoking Jesus and his disciples' experience of a storm on the Sea of Galilee (which we will look at on 10 September). As we were bouncing around rather uncomfortably in the large waves, a pod of pilot whales came and played in the waves breaking around our ship. This brought to mind the verse in this psalm about God forming Leviathan (a large sea creature) to frolic in the sea. The whales were ideally adapted to their environment and enjoying being in it.

   This psalm reminds us that not only did God create the creatures in the sea, echoing Genesis, but that he also cares for and provides for them. The sea does indeed teem with life, as the psalm says and as shown in the BBC TV series *Blue Planet*. God is sovereign over all the creatures in the sea, both giving them life and taking it away. Their lives are dependent on his provision of food for them at the proper time. Likewise, we too are dependent on God both for life and for food. It can be easy to forget at times that God is our provider, too.

God my provider, as your other creatures do,
help me to look to you for everything I need.

MERIC SROKOSZ

Evidence and the supremacy of Christ

He is the image of the invisible God, the firstborn of all creation; for in him all things in heaven and on earth were created, things visible and invisible, whether thrones or dominions or rulers or powers – all things have been created through him and for him. He himself is before all things, and in him all things hold together… For in him all the fullness of God was pleased to dwell.

The Christian faith is encapsulated in these stunning verses. Through Jesus' life, death and resurrection, all things – everything in the world as well as human beings – can be in a close relationship with God. But does the supremacy of Christ mean we should be able to obtain evidence of God's presence in the world? Although looking for this evidence was the expressed intention of early scientists, today the world can be almost completely described with the knowledge of science and mathematics alone.

But there is no need to give up looking for the evidence for God; instead, we need to redefine what we mean by 'evidence'. The word 'science' comes from the Latin *scientia*, meaning 'to know', whereas the biblical word associated with knowledge is 'wisdom', which is more about how we use what we know to interpret the world around us.

If we look at the complexity of our world (perhaps the vastness of the universe or the intricacies of the insect world – anything really), we can reach for some scientific facts. But if we contemplate the world with the wisdom of the supremacy of Christ, then startling new evidence emerges – our experience of wonder, joy and awe when we are faced with the world uncovered by science. And this is the evidence we need to know the truth that all things in heaven and on earth are held together in God through Jesus Christ our Lord. Our awe at the evolution of species, our wonder at the organisation of ant societies – whatever it might be: this is the evidence that leads to deeper wisdom than facts can ever deliver. Christ is supreme over all the earth!

Creator God, grant me the wisdom to wonder and the faith to know that Christ reigns supreme today in my life and everywhere.

GILLIAN STRAINE

Discerning wisdom through playful, childlike enjoyment

The Lord brought me forth as the first of his works, before his deeds of old; I was formed long ages ago, at the very beginning, when the world came to be… Then I was constantly at his side. I was filled with delight day after day, rejoicing always in his presence, rejoicing in his whole world and delighting in the human race.

The speaker in today's passage is Wisdom personified. Biblical wisdom is about alignment with God's creational intent. An analogy may help to explain. While it is possible to use a guitar to draw water from a well, it is unwise (the Bible would say 'foolish' or 'vain') to do so, as the guitar-maker intended it for making music. But adding percussive accompaniment to strumming (say, by knocking on the guitar with your knuckles) is a wise way to develop the instrument's potential. Made in the image of God, human beings are charged with discerning God's intention and wisely developing the huge potential built into God's creation.

Our passage speaks of the primacy of Wisdom, who was 'formed… at the very beginning'. Wisdom takes precedence over knowledge. Success in searching for knowledge through science and other endeavours does not guarantee discerning the way of wisdom: knowledge can, and often is, used unwisely. How, then, is humanity to learn to discern Wisdom's way?

The Hebrew behind the phrase 'I was constantly at his side' is obscure. Some scholars suggest the translation 'I was a little child'. Moreover, 'rejoicing' translates a word that carries the connotation of playfulness. So Wisdom, the little child at the creator's side, laughs playfully as the panorama of creation unfolds in front of her. When my own children were very young, I noticed they often reacted with playful laughter as they encountered new facets of the world. An excellent way for us adults to school ourselves in discerning the way of Wisdom is to recover, maintain and cultivate a childlike, playful enjoyment of the wonder, diversity and intricacies of creation.

God our creator, who created the universe in wisdom, instil in us a sense of playful enjoyment of all of your works. Amen

WILSON POON

All creation praise!

Praise the Lord from the earth, you sea monsters and all deeps, fire and hail, snow and frost, stormy wind fulfilling his command! Mountains and all hills, fruit trees and all cedars! Wild animals and all cattle, creeping things and flying birds! Kings of the earth and all peoples, princes and all rulers of the earth! Young men and women alike, old and young together!

Psalm 148 is a wonderful hymn, in which all areas of creation are called on to praise the Lord. God is deserving of the praise of all creation, and all creation is able to offer praise. In some traditions, worship is understood to be the saying of prayers or the singing of hymns or worship songs – exclusively human activities. Psalm 148 shows us just how wrong that understanding is.

By being the creatures that God intended and by filling the world with beauty and wondrous diversity, the rest of creation is also able to praise God. Animals offer praise when they delight in their surroundings and in just being themselves. Inanimate creation, too, offers praise by being a testament to God's creating love.

Nature also assists us in our own praise of God. Nature can inspire feelings of awe and wonder, and psychological research has shown that experiencing such feelings can produce a sense of transcendence – connecting with something bigger than ourselves. For Christians, such experiences can move us to greater praise of God. Science gives us an added way to experience awe and wonder as we explore the vastness of creation across the universe; as we marvel at the complexity of the microscopic world; as disciplines like psychology and genetics teach us more about what it means to be human.

Praise is something we do in community – rich and poor, men and women, old and young, human and non-human creation together. The mutual flourishing and peace of all creation is true praise to the loving creator.

Lord, teach me to marvel at your love, that my life
may join with all creation in praising you.

JENNIFER BROWN

New beginnings

In the beginning was the Word, and the Word was with God, and the Word was God. He was with God in the beginning. Through him all things were made; without him nothing was made that has been made. In him was life, and that life was the light of all mankind. The light shines in the darkness, and the darkness has not overcome it.

Modern science can tell us a great deal about the beginning. We know when the earth, and even the universe, formed, and we know a great deal about how they formed, thanks to modern scientific developments. For example, the Large Hadron Collider, which occupies a tunnel 27 km in circumference beneath the Franco-Swiss border near Geneva, is one of the world's largest physics experiments, designed to help us understand what happened at the beginning of the universe. Equally, satellite Cassini probed Saturn's rings for 13 years in order to improve our understanding of the formation of our planetary system.

John's gospel gives us another angle on the beginning. It reminds us of the ancient story of Genesis, about a God purposefully and lovingly creating his world. The regular use of these verses in Christmas carol services reminds us that this is also the beginning of a new story, albeit connected to the ancient one. The new story is one of light shining into what sadly had become a darkened world and a place in which God's best purposes had become frustrated. This is a story of light challenging and overcoming the darkness around it.

This is also the story of God's creative Word making possible a work of re-creation and a new beginning. As we continue into John's gospel, we read how the one who in the beginning formed life is now the author of new life. This is important for those times when we long for a new beginning for ourselves or those close to us. In my work as a geochemist, I have observed some of the earliest traces of life on earth, formed 3.7 billion years ago. John is telling us that in God's new creative order, even more exciting new beginnings are possible.

---

*Thank you, Lord, for the possibility of a new beginning,
for myself and those around me.*

HUGH ROLLINSON

God as faithful creator

Then God said to Noah and to his sons with him, 'As for me, I am establishing my covenant with you and your descendants after you, and with every living creature that is with you, the birds, the domestic animals, and every animal of the earth with you, as many as came out of the ark. I establish my covenant with you, that never again shall all flesh be cut off by the waters of a flood, and never again shall there be a flood to destroy the earth.'

This passage describes God making a covenant with 'every living creature' and, as was common in the ancient world, views this as including creatures inhabiting the skies (birds) and land (domesticated and wild animals). The word translated 'covenant' here is used to describe a contract regulating the relationship between two parties. Throughout the Bible are records of various covenants between God and human beings, alone or as families or nations. As Christians, we are drawn into the new covenant, sealed by Jesus' life, death and resurrection. The covenant in Genesis 9 is unusual because God here promises something to 'all flesh', that is, including animals and not just humans.

Why does God not just make a covenant with Noah and his descendants – or perhaps with the humans and their domesticated animals that provide them with items necessary for daily life? The more biologists uncover of the natural world, the more they become aware of the interdependency within and among all living things. There are highly intricate and dynamic relationships within each living cell, between cells, between organs in bodies and between animals and plants, both as individuals and as whole populations. We are part of a web of life. God did not create us in isolation but as creatures embedded within a wider created order. Moreover, here and elsewhere in the scriptures we find evidence of the Lord's ongoing faithfulness towards all that lives, not just humankind.

Thank you, Lord God, that you care for and continue to support all that you have made. Help us, Lord, to consider how we should live in relationship with your wider world in a way that respects you and all your creation.

CHERRYL HUNT

God's good creation

Where were you when I laid the earth's foundation? Tell me, if you understand. Who marked off its dimensions? Surely you know! Who stretched a measuring line across it? On what were its footings set, or who laid its cornerstone – while the morning stars sang together and all the angels shouted for joy?… The earth takes shape like clay under a seal; its features stand out like those of a garment… Have you journeyed to the springs of the sea or walked in the recesses of the deep?

God is addressing Job, who had been through a terrible time, losing his wealth, health and all ten children. Job just wanted God to explain why the world could be so tough.

God's response is simply to point to the magnificence of creation which lies all around. Job 38—41 beautifully explains God's immense creativity, his power and his sovereignty. Every single thing in the entire universe was called into being by God himself, from the vastness of the stars to the smallest details of the birth of every baby goat (Job 39:1–3). Even the food the animals and birds eat is under God's sovereign care (Job 38:39, 41).

The earth is not just a random lump of rock hurtling through space: God himself is its creator. It is exactly the size he meant it to be. It is exactly where he meant it to be. Its mountains and valleys, its ocean depths and seas are just as he intended. And these things matter: they are what make the earth a habitable planet, a suitable home for people made in God's image.

I know as a geologist that if the earth had been a different size, or a different distance from the sun, or if it didn't have seas and mountains and valleys, it would almost certainly be a sterile, lifeless planet. We can thank God for his goodness in making such a wonderful home for us, one which God himself declared in the first chapter of Genesis as being 'very good'.

*Lord God, I ask that today you will make me grateful
for the wonderful world which you have created for us.
Help us to use its resources to serve you and others.*

ROBERT WHITE

God's power over creation

One day Jesus said to his disciples, 'Let us go over to the other side of the lake.' So they got into a boat and set out. As they sailed, he fell asleep. A squall came down on the lake, so that the boat was being swamped, and they were in great danger. The disciples went and woke him, saying, 'Master, Master, we're going to drown!' He got up and rebuked the wind and the raging waters; the storm subsided, and all was calm. 'Where is your faith?' he asked his disciples. In fear and amazement they asked one another, 'Who is this? He commands even the winds and the water, and they obey him.'

Some of Jesus' disciples would have been experts on storms. They had lived all their lives on the shores of Lake Galilee, seeing the wind rise and fall and sudden squalls coming across the water. They would have known the conditions that made for a sudden storm in that area. As fishermen, their lives would have depended on making good judgements about the weather.

So when Jesus suggested they cross the lake, did the disciples murmur that the weather looked a bit iffy, or was the storm that blew up a surprise even to them? Whatever the case, when the wind·came and the waves started to lash the boat, they knew they were in trouble.

Knowing how something works makes a miracle all the more awe-inspiring. Miracles don't have to defy science. A meteorologist might be able to explain how a storm could leave as suddenly as it arrived, but that wouldn't explain away what Jesus did. The wonder was that it stopped as soon as Jesus spoke. The disciples had become used to these 'coincidences' happening, and they weren't going to ignore this one.

When the disciples experienced the miracle of Jesus calming a raging storm with his words, they knew he was no ordinary man. They knew what they were about when it came to weather, and they knew that this was an act of God.

Thank you, Father, that you sent your Son to come into the world and reveal to us your awesome power over creation. Help us to have faith in you and your power to act today.

RUTH BANCEWICZ

Knowing the creator

The heavens are telling the glory of God; and the firmament proclaims his handiwork. Day to day pours forth speech, and night to night declares knowledge. There is no speech, nor are there words; their voice is not heard; yet their voice goes out through all the earth, and their words to the end of the world.

Some years ago my wife and I were holidaying in Croatia. From our balcony in the evenings, because we were far away from artificial light, we were able to see the night sky in all its splendour and to count shooting stars. In ancient Israel, there also would have been no light pollution, and the night sky would have been equally spectacular.

The psalmist says that the heavens declare the glory of God. They are silent, yet metaphorically they speak loud and clear, and they speak to people 'through all the earth' – even if today we need to escape to the countryside to get a clearer view. They provide universally available testimony to God's glory.

The psalmist had a much more limited view of the cosmos than we do today. For example, like many in the ancient world he imagined the heavenly bodies set into a metal dome over the earth called the firmament. Now we know that the universe is utterly vast, maybe 93 billion light years in diameter. We also know that there are over 100 billion stars in our own Milky Way galaxy and over 100 billion galaxies in the observable part of the universe. By astronomical standards the sun is a very ordinary star, yet it is an 865,000-mile diameter nuclear furnace that has been radiating 400 trillion watts of power for many billions of years. Do these facts make me less or more in awe of God, the majestic creator of it all? Well, obviously, more so.

Our Christian faith teaches us that God, the creator of this unimaginably vast cosmos, is the very same God who, in the person of Jesus Christ, took human flesh and became a vulnerable baby. He came to achieve for us what we could not do for ourselves: by his perfect obedience, cross and resurrection, he redeemed us from all our failures. Now isn't that awesome?

RODNEY HOLDER

Rest

Thus the heavens and the earth were completed in all their vast array. By the seventh day God had finished the work he had been doing; so on the seventh day he rested from all his work. Then God blessed the seventh day and made it holy, because on it he rested from all the work of creating that he had done.

Have you ever seen something so beautiful, so wonderful, that it took your breath away? You literally found yourself lost for words. It's not a new experience. We share it with people through the ages, both those who have faith and those who have none. Rather than taking away from this breathless sense of wonder, the view of heaven and earth that science provides deepens it. Microscopes and telescopes give sight beyond natural human senses, opening up the 'vast array' of creation from the smallest to the largest scales – a divine window.

Perhaps before heaven and earth, God too was lost for words. On each day of creation, God speaks. His word brings all things into being. Now, on the seventh day, he contemplates all of creation, beyond even the rich view that God's gift of science provides. There is no more speaking needed. It is complete. God rests. God rests his voice, a holy moment.

With the seeming fullness of our lives, we have lost something of knowing this rest of God. We fear silence, filling our lives with noise through our phones, smart devices and TVs. Yet, in sabbath silence, in those moments that take our words away, we share in the deep delight of God over all that he has spoken into being, including his delight over us.

Next time you see one of the beautiful images of creation that science gifts to us popping up on your smart phone, tablet or TV, share a moment of holy silence with God. He invites you to join his wordless delight over what he has made and to rediscover the value he places in all things – and the value he places in you.

Praise to you, creator God, for the wonder of creation. Thank you for sharing it with me. In the vastness of it all, help me to know you more and to know that you know me. Amen

DAVE GREGORY

Jesus' miracles in Matthew

Children have no difficulty believing in miracles. Pretty much everything is miraculous to a preschool toddler, in that their minds are not yet demanding a rational explanation for things. They work on trust. They have no idea how the sun manages to rise every morning, but they go to bed each night trusting that daylight will appear the next day. Then they go to school and start to learn things about our extraordinary solar system and how it works. All of us have been through this process of education, and we discover there is order, reason and logic in the laws of our universe.

Although our knowledge of how things work has expanded hugely in the past 2,000 years, nevertheless the people of Jesus' day still knew there were clear rules that governed the world they inhabited. Granted, there was much superstition, and there is some evidence that there were healers and exorcists operating, in the time of Jesus, but clearly Jesus' miracles were remarkable, and there are frequent references in the gospels that not only his teaching, but also his miracles, amazed the people (see, for example, Matthew 9:33).

Matthew gives us accounts of many of Jesus' miracles, and what becomes clear in his gospel is that these miracles came with a message, which could be summarised thus: there is more to this world than that which you can experience with your normal senses and understand with your finite minds. There is another world that has its own laws, and it is alive and active in this world: it is called 'the kingdom of heaven', and sometimes the activity of this kingdom appears to conflict with the laws of nature as we know them. To understand the laws of this world, said Jesus, you do not need great knowledge and understanding, but you need to activate a sense which is called 'faith'. And there is one sure method for activating faith, and that is to become like a little child (Matthew 18:3). In the coming two weeks we shall be studying many of Jesus' miracles as described by Matthew. It will in many respects be a tutorial on how to become like a child.

MICHAEL MITTON

Miracles beyond measure

Jesus went throughout Galilee, teaching in their synagogues and proclaiming the good news of the kingdom and curing every disease and every sickness among the people. So his fame spread throughout all Syria, and they brought to him all the sick, those who were afflicted with various diseases and pains, demoniacs, epileptics, and paralytics, and he cured them. And great crowds followed him from Galilee, the Decapolis, Jerusalem, Judea, and from beyond the Jordan.

This story comes immediately after the calling of the first disciples, and these disciples quickly come to realise that this rabbi they have chosen to follow is no ordinary rabbi. He is not only a great teacher, but he also possesses the most extraordinary powers, such that they witness things they never imagined: blind people seeing, deaf people hearing and people once lame now leaping with joy. It would have been truly astonishing. Those who were sick were, I suspect, not bothered by how this miracle man did his work; they were just delighted to be free of the ailments that had bound them and made life so miserable for them.

No doubt there were some in Jesus' band who advised him to tone down all the healing a bit. People were now travelling from far-off places, and the crowds were getting out of hand. And besides, many in the crowd wanted just a straight healing and had no interest in the message Jesus was trying to preach. Some disciples might have said to Jesus that it would be better for him to heal just a select one or two – those who clearly understood the teaching and would take their discipleship seriously. But Jesus took no heed of such advice. His miracles were wild and free, with no strings attached. And this was because there was one overarching message that was fundamental to the gospel he came to preach: that this kingdom of God was one of lavish generosity and grace. This was the scope of the love of God – it was without measure and was available to all. It was not conditional on the ticking of any religious boxes.

What do you think your reaction would have been
if you had been there to witness these miracles?

MICHAEL MITTON

The power of life

When Jesus had come down from the mountain, great crowds followed him; and there was a leper who came to him and knelt before him, saying, 'Lord, if you choose, you can make me clean.' He stretched out his hand and touched him, saying, 'I do choose. Be made clean!' Immediately his leprosy was cleansed. Then Jesus said to him, 'See that you say nothing to anyone; but go, show yourself to the priest, and offer the gift that Moses commanded, as a testimony to them.'

In the ancient world, leprosy was one of the worst diseases you could get. Once the ulcerated lumps appeared on your skin you would know the worst – you were ill (usually terminally so) with a disease that had the added horror of alienating you from the rest of society. The leper had to remove themselves from their community (Leviticus 13:46). It was illegal to greet a leper and completely forbidden to touch them. You had to be at least six feet clear of a leper, else you were also deemed unclean. Rabbis were strict in enforcing what they believed to be a sensible law to protect public health. Few seemed to consider what life might have been like for the poor sufferer.

In today's story Jesus is returning from his teaching in the sermon on the mount with a great crowd following him. But the crowd would have rapidly dispersed as soon as people caught sight of a leper making his way towards Jesus. Though many translations tell us the leper knelt before Jesus, the Greek word implies that he worshipped him. Matthew wants us to understand that this leper detected something divine in Jesus, and Jesus was always more interested in faith than rules, so in response he does something that would have astounded the crowd – he touched him, thereby rendering himself unclean. He was making clear that there was now a new covenant at work. In the old covenant, you touch a leper and you become unclean; in the new covenant, you touch a leper and they get healed. In the kingdom of God, the power of life is stronger than the power of death.

Lord, make me a channel of your life today.

MICHAEL MITTON

The cost of miracles

When Jesus entered Peter's house, he saw his mother-in-law lying in bed with a fever; he touched her hand, and the fever left her, and she got up and began to serve him. That evening they brought to him many who were possessed by demons; and he cast out the spirits with a word, and cured all who were sick. This was to fulfil what had been spoken through the prophet Isaiah, 'He took our infirmities and bore our diseases.'

These few verses tell us so much about the way Jesus worked his miracles. It seems that Peter has invited Jesus to his home, where his wife's mother is part of the household. Jesus sees her and notices that all is not well – she is running a fever, possibly a very serious one. Once again Jesus uses touch in a healing story, and in touching the hand of Peter's mother-in-law, power is released, and she is immediately healed – so much so that she is able to get up and help with the dinner. It is a wonderfully tender and homely story.

Jesus hardly has time to get his supper down before there are knocks at the door, for word has gone round that he is there. Well into the evening Jesus works miracles of deliverance and healing, and no doubt the town became filled with the sounds of laughter and delight as people found freedom and healing after being touched by him.

Matthew then gives us a quote from Isaiah 53:4, informing us that these miracles are a fulfilment of the ancient prophecy that the Messiah will in some way take on himself our illnesses. However you understand the meaning of this, there is a clear message here that these miracles cost Jesus something. Ultimately his ministry to humankind cost him his life. Matthew wants to make clear to his reader that he is not talking about an entertaining wonder-worker here, but the Son of God who has entered so deeply into our world that he has drawn to himself our hurts and pains. His motivation was deep compassion and a desire to reveal the heart of God.

*What does it mean to you that Jesus took your infirmities
and bore your diseases?*

MICHAEL MITTON

The laws of the unseen world

And when he got into the boat, his disciples followed him. A gale arose on the lake, so great that the boat was being swamped by the waves; but he was asleep. And they went and woke him up, saying, 'Lord, save us! We are perishing!' And he said to them, 'Why are you afraid, you of little faith?' Then he got up and rebuked the winds and the sea; and there was a dead calm. They were amazed, saying, 'What sort of man is this, that even the winds and the sea obey him?'

Several of the disciples were acquainted with the sudden storms that could turn a dreamy Sea of Galilee into a white-water nightmare. By their reckoning, Jesus, coming from Nazareth (a town far from sea or lake), would have little understanding of the vagaries of the weather patterns over this lake, and he was probably the least qualified in that boat to know how best to steer them out of the storm. Yet by now, they have seen enough of Jesus to know that the normal rules do not apply. For example, there is the well-attested rule that in a wild storm on a lake, normal people do not sleep, because such rocking and splashing would stir the most somnolent of passengers. And yet Jesus sleeps, which in itself is something of a miracle. This is because the world within Jesus, the one he calls the kingdom of God, is so secure that no insecurity in the outer world can shake it. The disciples are still living in reference to the outer, seen world, rather than the unseen world of Jesus' kingdom.

When, in desperation, they do wake Jesus, he shows surprise at their failure to grasp the dynamics of this kingdom. It is then the disciples' turn to be surprised as they watch this inland carpenter stand in their storm-tossed boat and issue orders to the wind and waves! But their astonishment must have been even greater when the storm actually obeyed his command. And their question uttered in the awesome post-storm silence is one that we must all answer: 'What sort of man is this?'

How can you deepen your confidence in the
unseen world of Jesus' kingdom today?

MICHAEL MITTON

Deliver us from evil

When he came to the other side... two demoniacs coming out of the tombs met him... Suddenly they shouted, 'What have you to do with us, Son of God? Have you come here to torment us before the time?' Now a large herd of swine was feeding at some distance from them. The demons begged him, 'If you cast us out, send us into the herd of swine.' And he said to them, 'Go!' So they came out and entered the swine; and suddenly, the whole herd rushed down the steep bank into the lake and perished in the water.

Yesterday's story left us with the question 'What sort of man is this?' Today's story offers us the answer but from a most surprising source – two demoniacs. The disciples are probably still shaking as they arrive at the lakeshore when a new storm greets them in the form of two men whose lives have been highly damaged due to an evil influence. Matthew is in no doubt that there is another unseen world apart from the kingdom of God, and it is a world of evil that is in direct conflict with Christ. Today's story makes very clear just which is the more powerful – the kingdom of God.

The two men had clearly had associations with evil that had terrible effects on their lives, turning them to violence. However, there was one consequence that is apparent in this story, and that is, they could see spiritual realities clearly. The one spiritual reality they see when Jesus walks up from the lake towards them is that he is the Son of God. There is then a conversation involving men, Jesus and demons, the result of which is the eviction of the demons from the men to a nearby herd of pigs.

Theologians have argued for centuries regarding the meaning of this. However, for those two men the theology was by the by. For the rest of their lives they were grateful to the man whose light was so bright that it shattered the darkness that bound them. In a world dreadfully troubled by evil, this story is a great encouragement.

Lord, let your light blaze through me today.

MICHAEL MITTON

Freeing the heart

And just then some people were carrying a paralysed man lying on a bed. When Jesus saw their faith, he said to the paralytic, 'Take heart, son; your sins are forgiven.' Then some of the scribes said to themselves, 'This man is blaspheming.' But Jesus, perceiving their thoughts, said, 'Why do you think evil in your hearts? For which is easier, to say, "Your sins are forgiven", or to say, "Stand up and walk"? But so that you may know that the Son of Man has authority on earth to forgive sins' – he then said to the paralytic – 'Stand up, take your bed and go to your home.' And he stood up and went to his home.

In this run of stories in Matthew's gospel, we have seen a steady assertion of Jesus' authority – over sickness, over creation and over evil. In today's story, the focus is on Jesus' authority over sin, and this is a tricky business when there are scribes around.

It starts as a regular healing story – a group of friends bring a paralysed friend along to Jesus in the hope that he will heal him. Jesus discerns that there is a root to this problem that is in the realm of guilt and shame. At some point in this man's life he did something, the guilt of which has literally crippled him. To release the healing, Jesus therefore pronounces that his sins have been forgiven. For the scribes, this presents a serious problem – only God can forgive sin, usually through the prescribed routines of sacrifice. They believe theirs is the holy way, only to be told by Jesus that their thinking is evil. To make it completely clear, Jesus asserts that he has the authority to forgive sins, and he demonstrates this by healing the paralytic.

Guilt is a powerful burden that can paralyse parts of our lives. Guilt assumes that there has to be a punishment to make amends. It says something about the paralytic in this story that he was able to push past all the guilt dynamics of the religious system to simply believe that a word from Jesus could free him. The major miracle happened in his heart, not his legs.

Is there any way in which you need the freedom of Christ today?

MICHAEL MITTON

The culture of the kingdom

Suddenly a leader of the synagogue came in and knelt before him, saying, 'My daughter has just died; but come and lay your hand on her, and she will live'... When Jesus came to the leader's house and saw the flute-players and the crowd making a commotion, he said, 'Go away; for the girl is not dead but sleeping.' And they laughed at him. But when the crowd had been put outside, he went in and took her by the hand, and the girl got up. And the report of this spread throughout that district.

As Matthew's work was read out to groups of new Christians, it must have been a source of great excitement. Here was a story of Jesus written by a converted tax collector, and it is one full of miracles. By the time they reached today's story, those early listeners would have been wide-eyed in amazement. It is one thing to heal the sick, but could anyone walking this earth actually have the power to raise the dead? Surely not! And yet Matthew tells of a synagogue leader who comes to Jesus to report the death of his daughter, and who trusts that one touch from Jesus can bring her back to life. Some of those first hearers of the story may well have laughed like the mourners outside the dead girl's home. But Matthew gives it to them straight: one touch of the hand of Jesus raises the girl from death.

It is perhaps the casual way that Matthew relates the story that is so surprising – could he not have put just a little more drama into it? Maybe he wants to convey that in the world of the kingdom of God, rising from death is normal and natural. Matthew is not interested in the sensational. He watched Jesus carefully and observed that the kingdom that Jesus preached and demonstrated is one where the core theme is life, resurrection and the overcoming of death and darkness. Matthew's aim is not to impress people with miracle stories, but to shift their thinking. He is drawing them into a culture where even the raising of the dead seems reasonable.

Lord, lead me into the reasonableness of your kingdom.

MICHAEL MITTON

Dealing with devils

After they had gone away, a demoniac who was mute was brought to him. And when the demon had been cast out, the one who had been mute spoke; and the crowds were amazed and said, 'Never has anything like this been seen in Israel.' But the Pharisees said, 'By the ruler of the demons he casts out the demons.'

In the first-century world in which Jesus ministered, there was no difficulty in believing in the existence of demons. There are many instances in the gospels of people being delivered by Jesus from demonic influences. In some cases, the demonic influence has caused a sickness. In today's story, the afflicted person was mute and when the demon goes, the person speaks. Those of Jesus' day would have accepted the dynamics of this easily. The question was not 'Do demons exist?' but 'Who has authority over demons?' Jesus made it very clear that he, and his followers who ministered in his name, had full authority over them.

Matthew's note about the amazed crowd tells us that such clear and powerful authority over demons was unusual, and this authority disturbs the Pharisees. To quell the growing enthusiasm of the crowd for Jesus, they promote their line – that Jesus is in league with Satan, and it's all a massive deception. Such a claim tells us how dark their minds have become.

Christians today are apt to slide to one of two extremes – either dismissing the whole thing as pre-Enlightenment superstition or blaming pretty much everything on demons. C.S. Lewis, in his preface to *The Screwtape Letters*, remarks that the demons hail a materialist and a magician with the same delight! It is hard to deny the existence of evil in our world today. The issue is the same as it was in Jesus' day – who has authority over it? Matthew makes clear that Jesus' authority over evil is supreme. In the chapter following this story, Matthew relates how Jesus sent his disciples to heal and deliver from evil. In many churches, at a baptism service the candidates promise to 'renounce evil'. Tackling evil is part of the call to follow Christ.

How might God call you to tackle evil today?

MICHAEL MITTON

Dogged humility

Just then a Canaanite woman from that region came out and started shouting, 'Have mercy on me, Lord, Son of David; my daughter is tormented by a demon'… He answered, 'I was sent only to the lost sheep of the house of Israel.' But she came and knelt before him, saying, 'Lord, help me.' He answered, 'It is not fair to take the children's food and throw it to the dogs.' She said, 'Yes, Lord, yet even the dogs eat the crumbs that fall from their masters' table.' Then Jesus answered her, 'Woman, great is your faith! Let it be done for you as you wish.' And her daughter was healed instantly.

This is a story that takes place outside Jewish territory, and it is likely that Jesus was here on retreat in preparation for the demanding journey to the cross. As Matthew relates the story, it sounds as though Jesus and the disciples did not want to be interrupted on their retreat. Further, the woman doing the interrupting is a Canaanite, an ancient sworn enemy of Israel. But she has heard reports of Jesus and his power over demons, and it is a demon-slayer that she needs, because her daughter is terribly plagued by evil.

Once again, as with the leper (Matthew 8:2), Matthew uses the word for worship (translated 'knelt' here) as he describes the approach the woman makes to Jesus, for she also detects something divine in him. Her desperate need gives her rugged persistence. Jesus throws her the usual line of his religion, that God will only favour those who follow the correct path. And he offers the old insult that Gentiles are dogs. He is being deliberately provocative. Most people would be greatly offended and respond with anger or would retreat. But this woman's response shows extraordinary qualities of humility, love and faith. Jesus could perceive such qualities in her, and he wanted his disciples to see that in this Gentile woman lay a depth of faith that was truly inspiring. It was in response to this faith that he heals her daughter.

Pride can so easily rob us of God's blessings, but humility opens the door of faith.

What did it cost the woman to be humble?

MICHAEL MITTON

A mountainside miracle

Then Jesus called his disciples to him and said, 'I have compassion for the crowd, because they have been with me now for three days and have nothing to eat; and I do not want to send them away hungry, for they might faint on the way.' The disciples said to him, 'Where are we to get enough bread in the desert to feed so great a crowd?' Jesus asked them, 'How many loaves have you?' They said, 'Seven, and a few small fish.' Then ordering the crowd to sit down on the ground, he took the seven loaves and the fish; and after giving thanks he broke them and gave them to the disciples, and the disciples gave them to the crowds.

This is the second of two food-multiplication miracles. The first (Matthew 14:13–21) refers to people sitting on grass, so takes place in spring. The second is in summer. According to Mark's version of this story (Mark 8:1–10), Jesus is in the Decapolis, a region of ten Greek cities that included a large number of Gentiles. Perhaps Matthew was deliberately linking the theme of the bread of the last story with this one. On this occasion, the Gentiles are receiving much more than crumbs!

The motivation for this miracle is clear: the compassion of Jesus. The verses preceding this story tell us that Jesus is on a mountainside and that great crowds have gathered because of his miraculous healing. This crowd therefore is full of delighted people cured of their ailments. Jesus might have slipped away with a sense of a job well done. However, he knows that even cured people need to eat. He knows that being cured of your illness is not enough – you need bread for the journey. There is a strong message in this story that curing sickness is not enough to thrive in this world – there needs to be proper sustenance. In this case Jesus miraculously provides literal sustenance. But Jesus longs for humans to be fed with good bread, not the wrong sort provided by the Pharisees (see Matthew 16:5–12). Even a little of his life-giving teaching goes a long way.

Lord Jesus, feed me this day with your life-giving bread.

MICHAEL MITTON

Miracles and motives

The Pharisees and Sadducees came, and to test Jesus they asked him to show them a sign from heaven. He answered them, 'When it is evening, you say, "It will be fair weather, for the sky is red." And in the morning, "It will be stormy today, for the sky is red and threatening." You know how to interpret the appearance of the sky, but you cannot interpret the signs of the times. An evil and adulterous generation asks for a sign, but no sign will be given to it except the sign of Jonah.' Then he left them and went away.

The Pharisees and Sadducees were sects who were bitterly opposed to each other on several matters, but their hostility to the life and ministry of Jesus drew them together in an unlikely partnership. He threatened the power of both of these influential groups, and they both have agreed that something must be done to stop him. Jesus is becoming much more popular than the leaders of these two sects, and one of the main reasons for this is that he is performing so many miracles. So they decide to test him by asking him to show them a miraculous sign. Matthew describes a similar situation in 12:38–45.

In both these confrontations, Jesus refuses to perform miracles to order. His miracles are motivated by compassion and are not done to impress people. Jesus knows that even if he were to perform a miracle there and then, his opponents would use it immediately to attack him.

In response, Jesus picks up their language of signs. He registers that God's creation is full of signs. But he knows that those with darkened minds are only interested in signs that justify their causes or convictions. They are not willing to be open to signs from heaven that might disturb them or cause them to change. Even miracles can be misunderstood by the closed mind. Jesus never gave in to the pressure to prove himself. Jesus' way was relational: he invited people into relationship with him, and, once in the flow of his love, the signs would start to make sense.

Lord Jesus, lead me close to your heart that I may learn
true wisdom and understand the signs of your kingdom.

MICHAEL MITTON

Faith-filled community

When they came to the crowd, a man came to him, knelt before him, and said, 'Lord, have mercy on my son, for he is an epileptic and he suffers terribly; he often falls into the fire and often into the water. And I brought him to your disciples, but they could not cure him.' Jesus answered, 'You faithless and perverse generation, how much longer must I be with you? How much longer must I put up with you? Bring him here to me.' And Jesus rebuked the demon, and it came out of him, and the boy was cured instantly.

This story comes after the transfiguration. Jesus has taken with him Peter, James and John, leaving the other disciples behind in the valley. While they are waiting, the disciples are approached by a man who tells them that his son is having terrible epileptic fits. He understands that Jesus has trained his disciples to do miracles (see Matthew 10), so he asks them to deliver his son from this fearful illness. The disciples try their best to cure the lad, but to no avail. Then Jesus and the other three arrive, and the man rushes to Jesus, essentially telling him that the disciples are not up to much, and asking him to now do the job properly. Jesus responds with some very harsh words and then proceeds to heal the boy of his epilepsy.

The disciples must have felt despairing! Not only were they failures, but they seem to have offended Jesus as well. In the following verses Matthew reports the conversation with Jesus afterwards, in which he tells them that the problem is not simply personal; it is to do with the faithless culture of the generation. He wants his disciples to break out of that culture, into the culture of the kingdom of God. Jesus' exclamation reveals that it was hard for him to live in a faithless culture. But because of his love for the people, he longed for them to discover his faith-filled culture. One of his tasks was to build a community whose default culture would be the kingdom of God, and that community is called the church.

What is your default culture? If you belong to a church,
how can you help it develop the culture of the kingdom?

MICHAEL MITTON

The miracle of generosity

The collectors of the temple tax came to Peter and said, 'Does your teacher not pay the temple tax?' He said, 'Yes, he does.' And when he came home, Jesus spoke of it first, asking, 'What do you think, Simon? From whom do kings of the earth take toll or tribute? From their children or from others?' When Peter said, 'From others', Jesus said to him, 'Then the children are free. However, so that we do not give offence to them, go to the lake and cast a hook; take the first fish that comes up; and when you open its mouth, you will find a coin; take that and give it to them for you and me.'

The collectors of the temple tax want to know if Jesus pays his taxes, and this precipitates a conversation between Jesus and Peter, in which Jesus alludes to the custom of the day that, when a king imposes taxes on his people, his family is exempt. As a child, Jesus recognised that the temple was his father's house (Luke 2:49), so on this basis, he was family and should be exempt. However, Jesus chooses to pay the tax because of another principle, which is to do with not causing a stumbling block to be placed in someone's way. Jesus knows how difficult humans find it to manage money, and his way is always to encourage generosity. So he tells Peter to pay the tax.

He instructs Peter to go back to his old job of fishing, the job that used to earn Peter a living from which he paid his taxes. Peter heads for the lakeshore, throws in his line and, sure enough, in the mouth of the caught fish there is the coin. Through this miracle Jesus is conveying that the paying of the tax is a choice to give, and when you get that attitude right in your heart, then you can expect God the Father to provide what you need. The miracle in this story is to do not only with God's provision, but also with a radical change in the heart's attitude to money – indeed to taxation. It is the miracle of the generous heart.

What is God saying to you about giving and generosity?

MICHAEL MITTON

The way of faith

And seeing a fig tree by the side of the road, [Jesus] went to it and found nothing at all on it but leaves. Then he said to it, 'May no fruit ever come from you again!' And the fig tree withered at once. When the disciples saw it, they were amazed, saying, 'How did the fig tree wither at once?' Jesus answered them, 'Truly I tell you, if you have faith and do not doubt, not only will you do what has been done to the fig tree, but even if you say to this mountain, "Be lifted up and thrown into the sea", it will be done. Whatever you ask for in prayer with faith, you will receive.'

We have become used to Jesus using his miracles for wonderful, life-giving events. Here, however, we have a miracle that is to do with death and destruction. Jesus comes across a fig tree that shows no sign of fruit and he is so upset that he curses it. At first sight, you can't help feeling a bit sorry for the fig tree!

When commentators get going on this story, they usually dig out important links with the forthcoming destruction of the great temple, which is always seen as a judgement of God upon a faithless community that rejected the Messiah. He is therefore using this fig tree as a warning, making clear to his disciples that there is little point in having a fig tree in your garden if it fails to produce any figs.

He then goes on to use a quite different metaphor about a mountain and the sea – a clear reference to the working of miracles. Perhaps at the heart of this story is a message from Jesus that is essentially saying, 'There is no point in having a structure of faith, if there is no faith to show for it.' And by faith, he means the kind of faith that is open to the miraculous, which is a world that human institutions cannot control. A religion bound by human controls is of little use to God. A belief in a God who works wild wonders is not an option – it is an essential part of our faith and witness.

Lord, I believe. Help my unbelief.

MICHAEL MITTON

Deuteronomy

St Augustine of Hippo (AD354–430) is quoted as saying, 'Love God, and do as you will.' The writer(s) of the book of Deuteronomy did not have quite the same outlook. To love God involved adhering to a plethora of rules and regulations – 613 in all – which covered every aspect of life. These included the very familiar ten commandments but also apparently obscure laws, such as 'You shall not plough with an ox and a donkey yoked together' (22:10, NRSV).

But to think that Deuteronomy is just a long rule book would be unfair; indeed, it would miss the point. Deuteronomy is a pivotal book of the Old Testament, because it marks a major watershed. The context of the book is both literally and metaphorically on the border between 40 years' wandering in the wilderness and settlement in the promised land – between landlessness and landedness. It is the foundation upon which Judaism as an organised and structured religion is based.

Scholars further suggest that it is essential for a basic understanding of the New Testament, because the gospels contain so many references to Deuteronomy. To give just one familiar example – when Satan tests Jesus in the wilderness, Jesus responds with passages from Deuteronomy.

In terms of the structure of the book, there are a variety of theories and different levels of complexity, but at its simplest, Deuteronomy is divided into four sections: the first three are addresses by Moses to Israel, and the final section concerns Moses' death and succession. The first address is chapters 1—4, which sets the scene by telling how Israel came to its present watershed place and moment. The second section is long, comprising chapters 5—28; it is here that we find all these rules listed. Moses' third and final address is given in chapters 29—32, and it concerns an additional covenant made between God and Israel in Moab. Finally, section four tells of Moses' death.

Deuteronomy is such a dense book; common sense dictates that in these short reflections we can only dip into it, but I hope that through them a little of the shroud of mystery is lifted.

GEOFFREY LOWSON

Having the builders in

The high priest Hilkiah said to Shaphan the secretary, 'I have found the book of the law in the house of the Lord'… Then Shaphan the secretary came to [Josiah] the king, and reported to the king, 'Your servants have emptied out the money that was found in the house, and have delivered it into the hand of the workers who have oversight of the house of the Lord.' Shaphan the secretary informed the king, 'The priest Hilkiah has given me a book.' Shaphan then read it aloud to the king. When the king heard the words of the book of the law, he tore his clothes.

Years ago, as part of some alterations to my house, I had an old fireplace removed. Behind the wooden surround we found old newspaper clippings, a couple of postcards and a letter, all dating from the 1930s. It was an exciting and mildly emotional glimpse into the past.

Josiah was king of Judah from 640–609BC, and in the eighteenth year of his reign he embarked upon a major project to renovate the temple. First he raised cash through taxes, and then he called in the builders. During the restoration work they found a scroll hidden in the walls. It was none other than an early copy of the core of what we now call the book of Deuteronomy, probably chapters 12—26.

Josiah did more than rend his garments. Immediately, he called a public meeting of both temple officials and the public at which he solemnly promised to keep the Lord's commandments and all the laws written in the book. Further, he declared that there would be a turning back to the ways of the true God: idols and any objects or customs associated with pagan gods would be destroyed, and the temple would become a worthy dwelling place for God.

And so this scroll touched off a wave of reform in the land – reform that was not only religious but social as well. Under the new laws of Deuteronomy, there was to be more justice for everybody. Having the builder in led to great changes!

Has there been a time when some physical or practical change
in your circumstances led to a fresh beginning?

GEOFFREY LOWSON

Woven threads!

These are the words that Moses spoke to all Israel beyond the Jordan – in the wilderness, on the plain opposite Suph… In the fortieth year, on the first day of the eleventh month, Moses spoke to the Israelites just as the Lord had commanded him to speak to them… Beyond the Jordan in the land of Moab, Moses undertook to expound this law as follows.

A long tradition holds that the first five books of the Bible (the Pentateuch) were written by Moses, and this tradition honours his highly esteemed position. However, standard thinking is that there were four threads of material, which, when woven together, give us the Pentateuch. These threads or sources were written at different stages between 1000 and 600BC; they are known as J, E, D (Deuteronomist) and P. (Let us not worry about what J, E and P stand for.)

Clearly this is an involved area of study, but, suffice it to say, J and E are narrative in nature – they tell the story of God's people in those years before they settled in the promised land. D and P, however, are more reflective and contain the practical details of the social, economic and organisational aspects of everyday life for the new promised land.

Deuteronomy beautifully and intriguingly weaves together three things – the narrative; the religious and theological foundations of Judaism; and the details of social and political reform. But at the core of all this is the reality of the one true God.

For 21 years I worked for the Anglican mission agency USPG. The job was multifaceted, but a core part of it was visiting, teaching and preaching in different churches – many hundreds over that time. I enjoyed that immensely, but much more importantly I always came away from a church having learned something. There were different styles of worship, different traditions, different theologies at work and different glimpses of God. But the common, golden thread, wherever I went, was the worship of our God. Over the years I was privileged to have that glorious tapestry revealed – lots of threads woven together. It is there for any of us to discover.

Open our eyes, Lord, to the richness of our faith.

GEOFFREY LOWSON

The problem of land

For the Lord your God is bringing you into a good land, a land with flowing streams, with springs and underground waters welling up in valleys and hills, a land of wheat and barley, of vines and fig trees and pomegranates, a land of olive trees and honey, a land where you may eat bread without scarcity, where you will lack nothing, a land whose stones are iron and from whose hills you may mine copper.

At the very beginning of Deuteronomy we read: 'Go in and take possession of the land that I swore to your ancestors' (1:8). The relationship between God's people and the land runs deep in the Old Testament, but there are two strains of understanding.

One strain is the nomadic – the Abrahamic figure represents that wandering people of God who were willing to up sticks and move from place to place at God's will, all the time seeking a new land. The other strain is illustrated in the passage above. It is about being rooted in one place, a place promised by God where the people can settle for a good life: a land just for them.

But there is a problem. I have heard this passage at Harvest services all my life, and I have always found it very beautiful. Yet the theology and sentiment behind it have ramifications in the Middle East even today. Furthermore, many of the conflicts in the world today arise from the fact that people regard land as theirs and theirs alone. This issue of land is much too complex to deal with here, but if nothing else perhaps we can remember that for God, land was and is a gift.

And thinking about the two strains of understanding noted above, what of us as Christians? There is an undoubted tension – on the one hand we all find ourselves in a particular place with a responsibility to and for that place, but on the other hand we are meant to see ourselves as a pilgrim people, which involves movement.

To what extent are we prepared to be on the move as Christians,
if not physically, at least in terms of our thinking?

GEOFFREY LOWSON

Cutting a deal

Moses convened all Israel, and said to them: Hear, O Israel, the statutes and ordinances that I am addressing to you today; you shall learn them and observe them diligently. The Lord our God made a covenant with us at Horeb. Not with our ancestors did the Lord make this covenant, but with us, who are all of us here alive today. The Lord spoke with you face to face at the mountain, out of the fire… And he said…

I wonder if you can bring to mind some occasion when, along with others, you were called together for some important announcement. I can think of several, some more dramatic than others. The passage above is the introduction to one such grand announcement. In the simple structure of Deuteronomy (outlined in the Introduction, p. 35), this is the beginning of Moses' second address, and what follows the end of the quotation above is a listing of the ten commandments, or the Decalogue.

But back to the verses above, and three things warrant comment. The first verse is direct and firm: in introducing the Decalogue and all that follows, there is the instruction to hear, learn and do – 'Hear… the statutes… learn them… observe them.'

Second, there is a reminder that although the original covenant at Horeb (i.e. Sinai) was given to the people 40 years earlier, it still held fast and indeed it does so for every generation, ours included.

Third, this is a good place to mention covenants more generally. We read 'God made a covenant', but in Hebrew a more literal translation would be 'cut' a covenant. In ancient times, covenant ceremonies were part of the political structure and not uncommon. Rather uncomfortably from our perspective, they usually involved cutting an animal in half. The parties to the agreement would walk between the two halves of the animal, symbolising the dire consequences of breaking the covenant. We still use the expression 'cutting a deal'. That is rather heavy going to think about, but it stresses the gravity of these words and all those that follow.

Lord, strengthen us in the covenants we have made.

GEOFFREY LOWSON

Packed with meaning

One of the scribes came near and heard them disputing with one another, and seeing that he answered them well, he asked him, 'Which commandment is the first of all?' Jesus answered, 'The first is, "Hear, O Israel: the Lord our God, the Lord is one; you shall love the Lord your God with all your heart, and with all your soul, and with all your mind, and with all your strength." The second is this, "You shall love your neighbour as yourself."'

There are 35 references to Deuteronomy in the New Testament, and Jesus quoted from it nine times. Today's passage is in all three synoptic gospels. The first commandment is Deuteronomy 6:4–5 and the second Leviticus 19:18.

Let's focus primarily on the former, for these verses which Jesus quotes are part of the Shema: the basic and essential creed of Judaism, which every devout Jew prayed every day and does to this day. Almost every word is packed with meaning. Throughout Deuteronomy there is reference to 'your' or 'our' God, emphasising the intimate relationship to the one God as opposed to other gods. And this God is the one who has to be heard: 'Hear, O Israel.'

In the Hebrew language of Deuteronomy, 'love' has deeper connotations than the English word; there is a sense of obedience as well as the notion of a treaty. To put it perhaps over-simplistically, we are not talking here of mere emotion, but something binding. As if to hammer the point home, this love has to be offered through the heart, which was thought of as the seat of the intellect; through the soul, which was to do with one's very being; and with might or strength.

Finally, what of this word 'neighbour'? This too is interesting. In Leviticus and Deuteronomy, the word was much more all-embracing and included all dwellers in the land. By the time of Jesus, hard-line rabbis had made the definition much narrower. Jesus' teaching was to widen it again, hence the story of the good Samaritan in Luke.

We pray for those who feel rejected as neighbours.

GEOFFREY LOWSON

Sharpening your axe

Take care that you do not forget the Lord your God, by failing to keep his commandments, his ordinances, and his statutes, which I am commanding you today. When you have eaten your fill and have built fine houses and live in them, and when your herds and flocks have multiplied, and your silver and gold is multiplied, and all that you have is multiplied, then do not exalt yourself, forgetting the Lord your God, who brought you out of the land of Egypt, out of the house of slavery.

There is a lovely story of a woodcutter who applied for a job on an estate; he was genuinely keen to share in the running of the place. He got the job, the manager gave him a new axe and off he went. The first day, the woodcutter felled 18 trees. 'Congratulations,' said the manager. 'Go on that way!' The woodcutter was motivated by these words, but the next day he felled only 15 trees, and on the third day only ten. 'I must be losing my strength,' the woodcutter thought. He went to the manager and apologised, saying that he could not understand what was going on. The manager smiled and asked, 'When was the last time you sharpened your axe?'

Deuteronomy is a busy book – all those hundreds of rules and regulations, all those expectations. But on the other side of the covenant there is the promise of a wonderful, fulfilling life in the promised land, a life like no other. The danger which Moses foresaw was that, in their fabulous new life, the people would forget God. Like the woodcutter, they would be so wrapped up in the day-to-day, so wrapped up in making a mark for themselves, that they would forget to give time to God.

It does not take a huge leap of imagination to apply Moses' exhortation to our own age. Many of us reading this will have, relatively speaking, eaten our fill; we will have fine houses and live in them; all that we have will have multiplied. It is so easy to forget God and his commandments.

How do we make time for God in our busy lives?

GEOFFREY LOWSON

Gather around, please

These are the statutes and ordinances that you must diligently observe in the land that the Lord, the God of your ancestors, has given you to occupy all the days that you live on the earth. You must demolish completely all the places where the nations whom you are about to dispossess served their gods, on the mountain heights, on the hills, and under every leafy tree. Break down their altars, smash their pillars, burn their sacred poles with fire, and hew down the idols of their gods, and thus blot out their name from their places. You shall not worship the Lord your God in such ways. But you shall seek the place that the Lord your God will choose out of all your tribes as his habitation to put his name there.

If it is indeed the case that the manuscript found bricked up in the temple was Deuteronomy 12—26 (see reading for Sunday 27 September), it follows that these were the first words King Josiah had read to him by his secretary. The passage launches straight into one of the main underlying themes of Deuteronomy – the abandoning of all worship of other gods and a focus upon the one true God, including the centralisation of worship in 'the place that the Lord your God will choose', that is, Jerusalem. We need to read this bit of narrative from two different contexts.

First, at the time of Josiah, worship of pagan gods was rife. People practised idolatry. Just outside the walls of Jerusalem there was an altar where people sacrificed their firstborn child to the god Molech. There was even a shrine to an Assyrian god in the temple. Josiah had been anxious to rid his kingdom of all that; this manuscript was heaven-sent.

Second, Moses wanted to prepare the people for the transition from a nomadic life to a stable one, with worship in a central place. Instructing the people to 'seek the place' that will be God's habitation is a way of involving the people in this action.

Reflect upon this. We tend to be very attached to our places of worship, but in the Tyne Valley there is an initiative called 'God's Tent'. Each month it moves to a different place and people gather to worship and share.

GEOFFREY LOWSON

Foreigners and aliens

Every seventh year you shall grant a remission of debts. And this is the manner of the remission: every creditor shall remit the claim that is held against a neighbour, not exacting it from a neighbour who is a member of the community, because the Lord's remission has been proclaimed. From a foreigner you may exact it, but you must remit your claim on whatever any member of your community owes you.

Jubilee 2000 was a church-led campaign in the 1990s which called for relief of the debt that was crippling many developing countries. It was successful up to a point, in that it led to the cancellation of more than $100 billion of debt owed by 35 of the poorest countries. The two men who initiated the campaign were motivated by this passage and similar ones in both Deuteronomy and Leviticus.

In the Deuteronomic expression of the law, there was a deep concern for the welfare of all individuals, but especially the underprivileged and those in difficulty. This law was for those who found themselves in debt, particularly with respect to the land, but later in the chapter there is reference to the release of slaves too.

It is worth noting that this little passage is a good illustration of the way in which much of Deuteronomy is structured. First, there is a crisp statement of the law, then there is an explanation of how the law is to be carried out, and finally there is an expansion of the basic law.

This leads us to a matter of both interest and importance. 'From a foreigner you may exact it': this sounds harsh! In the Hebrew, however, the 'foreigner' is distinct from the 'alien' (or 'sojourner'). The former was one passing through Israel, perhaps on business, someone not integrated into the community. The latter referred to those from other places who had settled in and become part of the community.

There are many in our country who are 'aliens'
in the Deuteronomic sense of the word. We pray for them.

GEOFFREY LOWSON

Leftovers

When thou cuttest down thine harvest in thy field, and hast forgot a sheaf in the field, thou shalt not go again to fetch it: it shall be for the stranger, for the fatherless, and for the widow: that the Lord thy God may bless thee in all the work of thine hands. When thou beatest thine olive tree, thou shalt not go over the boughs again: it shall be for the stranger, for the fatherless, and for the widow. When thou gatherest the grapes of thy vineyard, thou shalt not glean it afterward: it shall be for the stranger, for the fatherless, and for the widow.

As children, my friends and I would scour the area looking for empty glass fizzy-pop bottles. We would then take them to the village shopkeeper, who would give us a few pennies in return. We were doing a bit of gleaning, gathering up what others had left behind. Perhaps returnable bottles might not be a bad idea in this generation.

One of the loveliest stories in the Old Testament involves Ruth gleaning in Boaz's fields after she and Naomi returned from Moab. The right to glean is one of a series of statutes designed to protect people from poverty, particularly the weaker members of society. Two other areas addressed in the preceding verses concern the just approach to loans and the prompt payment of wages.

A further important bit of background information here. We have noted earlier that a major emphasis in Deuteronomy is the leaving behind of other gods and a turning towards the one true God. In the ancient world it was the custom to leave some of the crops for the deities and spirits of the fields. This statute, then, as well as looking to the poor, was designed to shift the people away from those old practices.

Finally, why quote from the King James Version for this passage? The phrase 'all the work of thine hands' rather loses its impact in modern translations, where it reads 'all you undertake'. It appears several times in Deuteronomy, and it is Moses pointing to a settled agricultural life as opposed to the nomadic.

Lord, teach us to share our blessings.

GEOFFREY LOWSON

What on earth?!

You shall not muzzle an ox while it is treading out the grain. When brothers reside together, and one of them dies and has no son, the wife of the deceased shall not be married outside the family to a stranger. Her husband's brother shall go in to her, taking her in marriage, and performing the duty of a husband's brother to her, and the firstborn whom she bears shall succeed to the name of the deceased brother, so that his name may not be blotted out of Israel... You shall not have in your bag two kinds of weights, large and small.

Deuteronomy 21—25 contains a collection of apparently random laws; indeed, the three above have no obvious connection. Some are odd in our eyes because the cultural context is so unfamiliar, but there are some broad areas that cover purity of land and people, marriage and family, and the protection and care of others. The rule about the wife of a deceased brother is about the purity of the family line; the law concerning weights and measures is to guard against exploitation in the marketplace.

Let us look rather more closely at verse 4. Oxen pulling a sledge were used to loosen the grains of corn from the stalks. At one level this law may have simply been about kindness to the animal; there are other like-minded passages (Deuteronomy 22:6 has the most delightful reference to not disturbing a bird and her chicks in the nest). But it also seems to be about the ox sharing in the bounty of creation. The apostle Paul writes, 'It is written in the law of Moses, "You shall not muzzle an ox while it is treading out the grain." Is it for oxen that God is concerned? Or does he not speak entirely for our sake? It was indeed written for our sake, for whoever ploughs should plough in hope and whoever threshes should thresh in hope of a share in the crop' (1 Corinthians 9:9–10). Paul is speaking of both spiritual and material rewards. The oxen rule is an example of *a fortiori* – a lesser matter being used to make a greater point.

We pray for a fair and just sharing of rights and resources throughout the world.

GEOFFREY LOWSON

The juiciest and the best

When you have come into the land that the Lord your God is giving you as an inheritance to possess, and you possess it, and settle in it, you shall take some of the first of all the fruit of the ground, which you harvest from the land that the Lord your God is giving you, and you shall put it in a basket and go to the place that the Lord your God will choose as a dwelling for his name… You shall set it down before the Lord your God and bow down before the Lord your God.

When I was a child in the 1950s, my father worked in a fruit and vegetable warehouse, and every Saturday lunchtime he would arrive home from work with carrier bags full of potatoes, carrots, sprouts, turnips, apples, oranges, pears and so on – quite legitimately, for they were part of his wages! Over the seasons we were treated to most things.

I love Harvest services. The highlight for me is the bringing of gifts to the altar, which is a re-enactment of today's beautiful passage. But note that the passage firmly specifies that the offering was to be 'the first of all the fruit'. It is worth reflecting upon the gravity of that. God had to come first; God had to be offered the juiciest and the best olives, grapes, dates and figs, not the leftovers.

What has this to do with my father's bags of fruit and veg? In this present age we can go to the supermarket and get anything we want all year round. Strawberries at Christmas? No problem! The idea of the first fruits does not resonate in the same way today. In the 1950s, however, fruit and veg were seasonal: the first lettuce in May, the first strawberries in June, Cox's apples in September, new potatoes in October and so on. The first fruits of the season meant something.

What happened to the offerings specified in Deuteronomy? They were shared with the poor and the aliens and they had a party (26:11–12). Brilliant.

---

*Creator God, we thank you for the fruits of your creation
that are for both our sustenance and our pleasure.*

GEOFFREY LOWSON

Sign up and choose life

I call heaven and earth to witness against you today that I have set before you life and death, blessings and curses. Choose life so that you and your descendants may live, loving the Lord your God, obeying him, and holding fast to him; for that means life to you and length of days, so that you may live in the land that the Lord swore to give to your ancestors, to Abraham, to Isaac, and to Jacob.

Deuteronomy 29 begins: 'These are the words of the covenant that the Lord commanded Moses to make with the Israelites in the land of Moab, in addition to the covenant that he had made with them at Horeb.' Moses was to facilitate a second covenant. Why a second one?

The answer seems to lie in the fact that the people were poised on the border, and the time had come for some serious commitment. In return for 'loving the Lord your God, obeying him and holding fast to him' (v. 20), God is promising the people a rich and wonderful life in their new land over the border. The exhortation is to sign up and 'choose life' (v. 19).

It is important to note that on two other occasions when covenants are mentioned and choices have to be made (Exodus 19:3–9; Joshua 24:15–24), we read that the people made a positive response. In Deuteronomy, however, this is not the case; there is just silence. The significance of that silence is to leave the decision open; the response is not a past act, but it is to be given there and then by those who hear and receive the words. And this is intended to include us today. Are we prepared to make that positive response and sign up?

When I was a parish priest and had meetings with colleagues, the notion of commitment cropped up endlessly. We were talking of the few who were and the many who were not. This is a wider issue beyond the church: how do you get people to commit?

Pray for commitment in the life of the church.

GEOFFREY LOWSON

He will be with you

Then Moses summoned Joshua and said to him in the sight of all Israel: 'Be strong and bold, for you are the one who will go with this people into the land that the Lord has sworn to their ancestors to give them; and you will put them in possession of it. It is the Lord who goes before you. He will be with you; he will not fail you or forsake you. Do not fear or be dismayed.'

In 1872, a young Edward Steere found himself in charge of the UMCA mission station on Zanzibar. His bishop, William Tozer, had returned to England through ill health. A request came to staff a station in the Usambara Mountains on the mainland, so Steere commissioned four young men to go there.

The charge he gave them is both moving and profound. While it focused on the importance of integrating with the local culture, Steere also highlighted the partnership between the young men and God: 'You are sent as God's messengers to tell them what he has done for them. If none will receive your message, still God's part has been done, and you will have done yours if you have faithfully declared it. You will not be asked on the last day, "How many converts have you made?"… Do not grow weary in well-doing. God is with you and though you may see no result, your labour is not in vain.' (Clergy, take comfort!)

Tomorrow we will read of Moses' death, but today we think about what in modern parlance is referred to as 'succession planning'. God had prepared Moses for the fact that he would not lead the people into the promised land, and so here we have Moses giving Joshua his charge.

It is interesting that this pattern of commissioning is familiar in the Old Testament. First, there are words of encouragement ('Be strong and bold', v. 7), then a description of the task, and finally there is what scholars refer to as the assistance formula ('He will be with you', v. 8).

---

*We pray that God will be with us as we share
in the furtherance of the kingdom.*

GEOFFREY LOWSON

To the border

Then Moses went up from the plains of Moab to Mount Nebo… The Lord said to him, 'This is the land of which I swore to Abraham, to Isaac, and to Jacob, saying, "I will give it to your descendants"; I have let you see it with your eyes, but you shall not cross over there.' Then Moses, the servant of the Lord, died there in the land of Moab, at the Lord's command. He was buried in a valley in the land of Moab.

This is such a moving scene. Moses, now an old man, had worked so hard. He had risked so much and had suffered greatly at the hands of a people who never stopped complaining. He saw the vision of what was to be, yet the best he got was to view it from a mountaintop.

By the time we get to this point in Deuteronomy, we should not really be surprised by this ending, because in four earlier chapters we are told that Moses would not live to get to the land. The reasons given vary, because some of the text is from D and some from P.

It is the destiny of some to see the vision from afar, to be aware of what needs to be done, to set things in motion, to struggle with those who don't see the point, but then leave the outcome to God. Was Moses' death without meaning? Of course not. He had done what he had been chosen to do. He had completed his task. He had taken the people to the border.

Reflect upon this little story from North America:
'One day a hunter stopped by a lake and, as he reached down
to splash his face, in the still water he saw the reflection of a beautiful
white bird. He looked up, but the bird was gone. The rest of his life was
spent in a quest to find the bird. He journeyed far and wide until one day,
when he was very old, he was resting and felt a tickle on his face. He
reached up; it was a white feather, and he died holding it.'

GEOFFREY LOWSON

Home

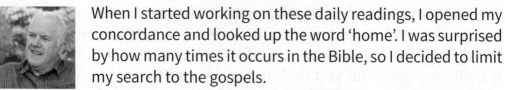

When I started working on these daily readings, I opened my concordance and looked up the word 'home'. I was surprised by how many times it occurs in the Bible, so I decided to limit my search to the gospels.

As I pondered, I began to see that the people we read of in the gospels had homes just like we have, homes that were important to them. That gave me an idea: I could focus on the different homes mentioned and see the story through the lens of the house. This would not be 'through the keyhole' exactly, but another way of seeing the story.

Let me introduce you, then, to some of the homes of people you will be familiar with, some rich, some poor. Hopefully it will help you to think about your own home, what it means to you and how God might want your faith to impact you where you live.

TONY HORSFALL

Zechariah's home

At that time Mary got ready and hurried to a town in the hill country of Judea, where she entered Zechariah's home and greeted Elizabeth. When Elizabeth heard Mary's greeting, the baby leaped in her womb, and Elizabeth was filled with the Holy Spirit. In a loud voice she exclaimed: 'Blessed are you among women, and blessed is the child you will bear!'

At the time of Jesus, some houses in hilly regions were partial cave dwellings, built up against the rock face with a front section added on. These structures were easy to build and had a natural coolness to them. Perhaps this was the kind of home that Zechariah the priest and his wife Elizabeth enjoyed.

Into this simple home they were glad to welcome Elizabeth's cousin Mary in her hour of need. She had felt the need to get away from Nazareth for a time during her pregnancy and to ponder God's purpose for her life. But where to go? She immediately thought of her elderly relatives. Elizabeth had her own story of God's intervention, and we can imagine how much the two had to share, talking long into the night.

The godly Elizabeth was able to encourage her young cousin with words from God. Her sensitivity to the voice of God marks her out as a wise and mature believer. The time given to listening to Mary made the mother-to-be feel safe and secure, exactly what she needed. How fondly Mary would have remembered her three months in the Judean hillside.

Elizabeth gives us a good example of what it means to mentor another person, to be a 'mother' in God to someone who needs help and encouragement. Gladly she gave her time and made room in her life for Mary. Even a simple home can be a safe place when there is welcome and a sense of acceptance. Be on the lookout for anyone whom God may bring into your life at a time of need.

Lord, give me eyes to see those in need
and a word of encouragement to share with them.

TONY HORSFALL

Simon Peter's home

As soon as they left the synagogue, they went with James and John to the home of Simon and Andrew. Simon's mother-in-law was in bed with a fever, and they immediately told Jesus about her. So he went to her, took her hand and helped her up. The fever left her and she began to wait on them.

Italian excavators working in Capernaum have uncovered what is believed to be the remnants of the house where Simon Peter lived with his extended family, and which became a home to Jesus. Buried beneath the remains of an octagonal Byzantine church they found the ruins of a mundane dwelling dating from the first century BC. Like most houses of the period, it consisted of a few small rooms clustered around two open courtyards.

The relationship between Jesus and his first disciples here was still in its embryonic stage. He had met the four fishermen by the Sea of Galilee and invited them to follow him. They joined him in the synagogue at Capernaum and had witnessed the deliverance of a man possessed by an impure spirit. No doubt that grabbed their attention. It seemed natural to invite him back home afterwards for something to eat.

The domestic crisis that greeted them must have taken Simon by surprise. His reaction is instructive: his automatic response was to tell Jesus about his mother-in-law. Did he instinctively feel that Jesus could help? If so, his instinct was correct, for Jesus goes to her, helps her up and the fever is gone. A very ordinary miracle, in a very ordinary home, on a very ordinary occasion.

This first healing miracle is nothing spectacular. It reminds us that we should bring our very ordinary needs to Jesus without hesitation. Healing a fever (malaria?) is like healing a common cold, and both are valid concerns to share with the Saviour. It is in these small interchanges that faith is built up and the power of God realised. Miracles happen at home as well as in church.

Lord, thank you that you are willing to demonstrate your power
in the mundane concerns of our ordinary lives.

TONY HORSFALL

A home filled with praise

'Which is easier: to say, "Your sins are forgiven," or to say, "Get up and walk"? But I want you to know that the Son of Man has authority on earth to forgive sins.' So he said to the paralysed man, 'I tell you, get up, take your mat and go home.' Immediately he stood up in front of them, took what he had been lying on and went home praising God.

The story of the paralysed man is well known for the fact that his friends broke through the roof of the house to lower him down in front of Jesus – such was their desperation and determination that he should be well again. We may wonder at such destructive behaviour, but the damage was probably not as great as we might think. The roof would have been made of wattle or straw mats covered over and smoothed with hard clay – easy to break through and easy to repair.

What we notice here is not the damage done to the first house but the joy restored to the second house – the home of the paralysed man. The one who had been carried by his friends to meet Jesus now returns home under his own steam, no doubt walking and leaping and praising God – like the man at the Beautiful Gate (Acts 3:8). What a transformation in his life, the result of his encounter with Jesus.

Have you ever noticed how every home has an atmosphere of its own? For example, some feel very peaceful and calm, while others are chaotic and noisy. Perhaps the paralysed man's home had been full of sadness, a quiet despair seeping into everything, given his tragic circumstances. Now all that is gone, replaced by joyful praise to God. Thankfulness and gratitude fill the air. The atmosphere is impregnated with hope and optimism. You feel it as soon as you enter the house, and it is contagious – 'everyone was amazed and gave praise to God' (v. 26).

I wonder what people sense when they enter our home. Is it something of the presence of God – his peace, his love and his joy?

Lord, may the fragrance of Jesus fill my life and my home.

TONY HORSFALL

The home of Jairus

He did not let anyone follow him except Peter, James and John the brother of James. When they came to the home of the synagogue leader, Jesus saw a commotion, with people crying and wailing loudly. He went in and said to them, 'Why all this commotion and wailing? The child is not dead but asleep.' But they laughed at him.

Religious homes, rightly or wrongly, are often portrayed in books and films as being strict and joyless, with little room for personal freedom. Those who, like Jairus (a synagogue official), carry heavy responsibilities for communicating religious truth and upholding moral standards sometimes become overbearing at home, even when it is not their intention. I can imagine Jairus making sure his family carefully followed all the Jewish regulations and traditions, but I don't get the impression that he was a harsh man. His love for his daughter shines throughout this story of grace, along with his faith, humility and spiritual awareness.

In his desperation to find healing for his daughter, Jairus throws himself on the mercy of Jesus, despite knowing this would place him at odds with the other religious leaders. When Jesus eventually arrives at Jairus' home, he encounters in the professional mourners a wall of cynical unbelief and hopeless despair. The sense of grief and loss is palpable, and in order to facilitate the work of God these scoffers are sent away. Significantly, Jesus takes the parents and his disciples into the sick room with him, presumably because of their faith. There the child is restored to life.

Here is a home that from this moment on is characterised by grace and faith. The joyful vitality of a healthy teenage girl fills the place, but more than that, the spiritual vitality of a living faith in God is in evidence in how the family lives together. Through Jesus they have found true freedom and joy.

How might your home become a place of faith rather than of unbelief?

Lord, guard us from religiosity and legalism. May our hearts and our homes be filled with your love and grace.

TONY HORSFALL

Home-based witness

As Jesus was getting into the boat, the man who had been demon-possessed begged to go with him. Jesus did not let him, but said, 'Go home to your own people and tell them how much the Lord has done for you, and how he has had mercy on you.' So the man went away and began to tell in the Decapolis how much Jesus had done for him. And all the people were amazed.

I have the rather unusual distinction of living just a couple of miles away from where I grew up. I often pass the houses where variously I was born, was a teenager, lived when first married and raised a family of my own for over 20 years. Although I have travelled far, I find myself once again back home.

The call to 'go home to your own people' is not an adventurous one. Indeed, the man in this story, who had been dramatically set free from the demons that had tormented him, is acutely disappointed that he cannot join Jesus on the road. He would love to share his amazing story in more exciting locations. Instead, he is sent back home to his own people.

Why was this? Primarily because he would have a unique testimony to share among his own people. The region of the Gerasenes was off the beaten track on the eastern shore of the Sea of Galilee, a mostly Gentile region where the light of the gospel was desperately needed. Here the dramatic nature of what God had done for the man would be appreciated, since they themselves had witnessed his afflictions and could see first-hand the dramatic transformation in him. He knew their culture, could speak their language, was one of their own and was therefore ideally placed to share the good news.

It is never easy to witness to our own people, but sometimes 'home' is where we are called to be, and we should not underestimate the opportunity or devalue such a calling. Wherever God has placed us we can tell how much the Lord has done for us.

Lord, let me shine brightly for you in the place which is now 'home'.

TONY HORSFALL

Coming home seeing

After saying this, he spat on the ground, made some mud with the saliva, and put it on the man's eyes. 'Go,' he told him, 'wash in the Pool of Siloam' (this word means 'Sent'). So the man went and washed, and came home seeing. His neighbours and those who had formerly seen him begging asked, 'Isn't this the same man who used to sit and beg?'

This is a most remarkable miracle, accompanied by some unusual actions on the part of Jesus. After all, spitting is not a very acceptable thing to do. The miracle also plunges the man who is healed into the midst of a fierce controversy, where his integrity is questioned by the powerful and intimidating Pharisees who are determined to prove that Jesus is a charlatan.

I can only begin to imagine what it is like to be able to see after having spent your whole life in darkness. It must be amazing, but also a little disorientating and confusing, as you try to make sense of a world you can now see. The home this man once knew only through touch he can now see and enjoy for the first time. No more banging into things; no more feeling his way around. His neighbours cannot believe it is the same person, but his testimony is sure: 'One thing I do know. I was blind but now I see!' (v. 25).

There is, however, a deeper layer to this story. Blindness is not only physical; it can also be spiritual. The Pharisees, for all their understanding and knowledge of tradition, cannot see that Jesus is the Son of Man and that the healing is an act of God. Here is the irony: a blind man is made to see, while those who can see become blind (v. 39). They cannot see because they don't want to. They create their own blindness.

The man in this story is healed twice, first of his physical blindness, then of his spiritual blindness. His response to Jesus is remarkable: 'Lord, I believe,' he says, and he worships him (v. 38).

Lord, you have opened my eyes. Now help me to see you
in the world around me and in the people I meet.

TONY HORSFALL

Open home

As Jesus and his disciples were on their way, he came to a village where a woman named Martha opened her home to him. She had a sister called Mary, who sat at the Lord's feet listening to what he said. But Martha was distracted by all the preparations that had to be made.

Homes are characterised by the people who live in them – think of student accommodation, flats for elderly people or penthouse apartments for executives. Each will have its own style, unique décor and furnishings.

So what of the house at Bethany where the three siblings Mary, Martha and Lazarus lived together? I imagine it to be a tidy, well-run house with clearly defined responsibilities. We know little of their backgrounds or why they appear to be unmarried, but they seem to have chosen to live together and to be happy with the arrangement.

This home in Bethany is what we often describe as an 'open' home, by which we mean it was given to hospitality. Friends and neighbours, and maybe strangers too, were welcome to drop in. The door was always open, as we say. The arrival of Jesus with his disciples was therefore not an unwelcome intrusion but a happy occasion for friendship and fellowship. This was a house where Jesus could relax and feel at home.

Hospitality is not the same as entertaining. Hospitality is about caring for people, not impressing them. Some people seem to have a particular gift for making others feel welcome and accepted, and they use their home to encourage and support others. It is a ministry in itself and a very valuable one. We may not all have this gifting, but we can all be hospitable in our own way, offering a welcome and a listening ear.

Churches too can practise hospitality, and members can be involved in offering a welcome to the lonely, the bereaved, the disadvantaged, the refugee and so on. Many town-centre churches provide lunches for students. One village church I know offers a free breakfast once a week to anyone who wants to come.

Lord, thank you for the blessing of my home.
Show me how it can become a place of ministry.

TONY HORSFALL

A fragrant home

While Jesus was in Bethany in the home of Simon the Leper, a woman came to him with an alabaster jar of very expensive perfume, which she poured on his head as he was reclining at the table. When the disciples saw this, they were indignant. 'Why this waste?' they asked. 'This perfume could have been sold at a high price and the money given to the poor.'

Bible scholars wonder about a connection between the house of Simon and that of Mary, Martha and Lazarus. It may be that Simon lived with them, a reflection of their gift of hospitality. Tradition suggests that Bethany was the site of an almshouse for the poor and a place of care for the sick. There may also have been a settlement for lepers, in which case Simon may have been a wealthy man who was healed of the disease and was now restored to society.

Whatever the background, Simon's home is the setting for a remarkable act of worship. The unnamed woman (perhaps Mary Magdalene) took one of her most precious and valuable possessions and lavished it upon Jesus as an act of love and devotion. Rationally, such an extravagant act seemed wasteful and imprudent, especially to the more money-conscious disciples. They clearly did not understand the power of gratitude or the motivation of love. This woman had been wonderfully set free by Jesus from a life of sin, and this was her way of showing her thanks.

As a result of her action the house was filled with a beautiful fragrance, the fragrance of passionate worship and extravagant love. Her sacrificial devotion had been released and its perfume could not be restrained. Jesus was deeply touched, seeing it as a preparation for his forthcoming death and describing it as 'a beautiful thing' (v. 10).

Perhaps in our desire to avoid extremes we can sometimes stifle any passion in worship. Our desire to always play it safe can mean we never really know what it is to be lost in wonder, love and praise. Is it time to break the jar and let the love begin to flow?

Lord, forgive me if I am too formal in my love for you.
Teach me to be more extravagant in my worship.

TONY HORSFALL

A shepherd's home

Then Jesus told them this parable: 'Suppose one of you has a hundred sheep and loses one of them. Doesn't he leave the ninety-nine in the open country and go after the lost sheep until he finds it? And when he finds it, he joyfully puts it on his shoulders and goes home. Then he calls his friends and neighbours together and says, "Rejoice with me; I have found my lost sheep."'

Farmhouses to my mind are never very tidy, especially the kitchen. They are more functional and pragmatic, a base for the hectic round of daily activities, a depository for things that need mending and things that may come in useful. I imagine a shepherd's home to be similar, often with an injured lamb wrapped in a blanket on the floor. Homes and occupations go together.

In this parable, Jesus imagines the care and compassion of the shepherd for one lost sheep. Although the shepherd has many other sheep, it is the one missing lamb that has his attention. In order to find the stray, he must leave the comforts of home and set out, whatever the weather and facing the danger of the wild countryside.

This is, of course, a picture of Jesus' own shepherd heart and an illustration of his love that brought him down to seek and to save that which was lost. It reminds us of the sacrificial love that took him to Calvary and of the grace that sought and found us in our need. Many of us can sing from our heart, 'I was lost, but Jesus found me' (F.H. Rowley, 1854–1952), and we have our own story to tell of wandering far from the shepherd's tender care.

Home can be such a wonderfully comfortable place that we never want to leave. One of the challenges of this parable is that sometimes we have to leave home comforts behind if the lost are to be found. Jesus left the glory of heaven on our behalf, and we too must be willing to put ourselves out for the sake of others. Mission may involve sacrifice; service can be costly.

Lord, I am so grateful that you found me. Help me now to seek others.

TONY HORSFALL

A tax collector's home

So he ran ahead and climbed a sycamore-fig tree to see him, since Jesus was coming that way. When Jesus reached the spot, he looked up and said to him, 'Zacchaeus, come down immediately. I must stay at your house today.' So he came down at once and welcomed him gladly. All the people saw this and began to mutter, 'He has gone to be the guest of a sinner.'

Wealthy homes in the time of Jesus had multiple storeys, extra rooms with a courtyard and lavish furnishings. No doubt some of Zacchaeus' wealth had gone into creating a nice home. To the rich, a home is a status symbol.

Beneath his successful exterior, however, it seems that Zacchaeus was a troubled man. Wealth cannot buy peace of mind, and perhaps the way he had gained his income troubled his conscience. Maybe it was simply that, having achieved his ambitions and risen to the top, he still felt empty and unfulfilled. Instinctively he was drawn towards Jesus, sensing that the Galilean might have the answer to his longings.

Zacchaeus was exactly the kind of lost sheep that the good shepherd had come to find. Jesus' ever-watchful eye saw the tax collector high in the tree and called to him to come down. Salvation was on offer if Zacchaeus would humble himself, come down from his perch and open his home to the Saviour. Sinner he may have been, but he was still loved and valued by God.

Jesus continually offers to meet with us, but his coming is conditional upon our being humble enough to admit our need and brave enough to welcome him into our lives. In 1951, a Presbyterian minister (Robert Boyd Munger, 1911–2001) wrote a little booklet called *My Heart – Christ's Home*. It became a classic explanation of what it means to bring every aspect of our lives under the leadership of Jesus. Munger tells how Jesus came into the darkness of his heart and turned the light on. He describes how Jesus built a fire in the cold hearth and banished the chill, filling the emptiness with his loving presence.

Perhaps Zacchaeus experienced something similar. You can too.

Lord, I open the door of my life to you. Come in, come in.

TONY HORSFALL

A home in the city

The women who had come with Jesus from Galilee followed Joseph and saw the tomb and how his body was laid in it. Then they went home and prepared spices and perfumes. But they rested on the Sabbath in obedience to the commandment. On the first day of the week, very early in the morning, the women took the spices they had prepared and went to the tomb.

For a number of years I led a mentoring programme in Singapore designed to help participants grow in their relationship with God. Early on I 'happened' to meet an Anglican minister and his wife who had recently refurbished their home so it could also be used for retreats. They suggested that we might hold our mentoring course there, and that I could stay free of charge whenever I was in the city. It was an amazing provision of God, and that house became a place of blessing to many over several years.

God blesses people with resources so they can use them for the benefit of others. Many have been able to offer their homes to God for him to use to refresh his people. The women from Galilee who followed Jesus to Jerusalem during his last days may have struggled to find accommodation had it not been for the generosity of an unknown benefactor who gave them use of a home in the city. It is a small detail in a much bigger story, but another example of Christian generosity and wise stewardship.

We can see from the story how much this borrowed home meant to them. Here was their place of refuge during a period of emotional turmoil. Here they could get to work on practical matters – preparing the spices with which to anoint the body of Jesus. Here too they could keep the sabbath and rest themselves physically. From here they set out for the tomb on the first Easter morning.

Is it possible that you may be able to offer your home for God to use in some way? Perhaps for hosting a home group or a quiet morning, or maybe as the venue for a prayer meeting or planning group?

Lord, all that we have comes from you. Help us to steward our possessions wisely, with generous hearts.

TONY HORSFALL

Finding a home

Near the cross of Jesus stood his mother, his mother's sister, Mary the wife of Clopas, and Mary Magdalene. When Jesus saw his mother there, and the disciple whom he loved standing near by, he said to her, 'Woman, here is your son,' and to the disciple, 'Here is your mother.' From that time on, this disciple took her into his home.

On holiday in Turkey I visited the ruins of Ephesus, and on the journey stopped at a location said to be the place where the apostle John lived together with Mary the mother of Jesus. A first-century house was discovered there in 1891 beneath the ruins of a fourth-century church, and since John was known to have lived in Ephesus, the connection was made. Ever since it has been a place of pilgrimage.

Here we see the tenderness of Jesus towards his mother, thinking of her welfare even as he dies on the cross. Was this an off-the-cuff decision or rather something Jesus had thought about and even discussed with John beforehand? It is unclear why Jesus (the eldest son) does not place Mary in the care of her other children. Perhaps there was already an affinity between Mary and John. It strikes me that Jesus knew this relationship would be mutually beneficial, since he addresses them both. Doubtless John would benefit from a mother figure, and Mary from John's protection.

Whatever the reason, John responded with obedience and welcomed Mary (already a widow) into his home, providing a safe place for her as well as food and lodging. This would be especially important as she grew older, and in this regard John's welcoming of Mary reminds us of all who are carers within their own home. Indeed, this incident suggests that a particular blessing rests on those whose life is given to caring for elderly or sick relatives at home.

Such a calling is not possible for all, hence the need for care homes and hospices. But those who find themselves in the position of carer can have a valid ministry and are worthy of our support and prayer.

Lord, bless all who give care at home.
Grant them strength, compassion and patience.

TONY HORSFALL

Taking Jesus home

As they approached the village to which they were going, Jesus continued on as if he were going further. But they urged him strongly, 'Stay with us, for it is nearly evening; the day is almost over.' So he went in to stay with them.

The story of the two disciples on the road to Emmaus is one full of significance. We are unsure of their exact identity and relationship. Was this a married couple, the Mary and Clopas mentioned in yesterday's reading? Or were they simply two friends joined together in their desire to follow Jesus as his disciples?

What is clear from Luke's account is that they had been terribly disappointed by the events in Jerusalem and, following the death of Jesus, were returning broken-hearted to their home in Emmaus. At this point they have still not recognised that the stranger who had joined them on the road was the risen Jesus, but they have enjoyed his company and invite him to stay the night with them.

Two things stand out here. In making as if to continue his journey Jesus is not assuming anything. He does not want to force himself upon them, but prefers that they genuinely desire his company. It is a little test for them. Jesus will never force himself on anyone. Always he waits for us to invite him in. We must choose his friendship.

Secondly, disciples are those who gladly welcome Jesus into the sphere of their daily lives. It is actually through an ordinary and homely activity – breaking bread – that Jesus becomes known to them (vv. 30–32). A simple meal together becomes a sacramental moment and a means of spiritual revelation.

Home is where we are most relaxed, where we are most fully ourselves. What a joy to know that Jesus is willing to join us in the ordinariness of our daily lives, where we can enjoy his presence in every aspect of life at home.

Lord, thank you for your willingness to make your dwelling among us,
even to the point of being present in our homes.

TONY HORSFALL

At home with God

'Do not let your hearts be troubled. You believe in God; believe also in me. My Father's house has many rooms; if that were not so, would I have told you that I am going there to prepare a place for you? And if I go and prepare a place for you, I will come back and take you to be with me that you also may be where I am.'

How do you imagine heaven? It is hard for anyone to truly grasp what heaven will be like. It will be beyond our wildest dreams, and better than we could ever have conceived. I like this picture (and it is a metaphor, remember) that Jesus gives us here of a mansion with many rooms, because it feels so homely. It will not be some vast, impersonal place where we feel lost and alone but somewhere we are known and loved, a place where we truly belong.

I have stayed with many families over my years of mission work and itinerant ministry, and I am grateful to have received so much wonderful hospitality. Every home has its unique elements and is an expression of the owner's personality and taste. 'My Father's house' will be no different. It will be packed with interest and beauty and will take our breath away. There will be so much to see and discover, so much that is new to us and that excites our wonder. It will be a joyous, happy place filled with fun and laughter. Above all it will be a home devoid of pain, suffering and mourning. There will be no crying and no more tears. So much for us to look forward to!

These words are meant to reassure our hearts and to comfort us in times of trouble. In this earthly life we do experience sadness and heartache, and no home is spared its share of woe. But when our home is filled with sorrow, we can always remember that we have another home to look forward to, a better home in heaven that is permanent and that even now is being prepared for us.

Lord, thank you for the reassurance that to be away
from the body is to be at home with you.

TONY HORSFALL

Galatians: the letter from Mr Angry

The apostle Paul is angry. This letter to the churches in Galatia is not warm and cosy; it's abrupt, fiercely confrontational and boiling with emotion. If you look at the beginning of Paul's letters, the initial greeting is usually followed by a strong affirmation of those to whom he is writing. Not Galatians. Paul can't manage a single good word for them. Instead, straight away, he gives them both barrels. Something terrible has happened. It's so terrible that Paul fears they are in great danger – in danger of turning away from the family of God that they had joined when they responded to Paul's preaching.

Luke tells us that Paul visited the southern part of the Roman province of Galatia (now central Turkey) on one mission trip (Acts 13—14) and the northern part on another (Acts 16:6). He seems to have established churches in both areas; his letter is simply addressed to the churches in Galatia. He obviously expected – or at least hoped – that his letter would be read and passed on, so that all would know of his anger and concern.

You could sum up Paul's message very crudely: I brought you good news; you are abandoning what I taught you; I'm the apostle; I'm right; and anyone who disagrees with me is not only wrong but also undermining the whole basis of Christian faith. It can read as if Paul has taken offence because his teaching is being rejected, as if it is all about Paul and his damaged ego.

But as we shall see, Paul's anger stems from the fact that he has brought them good news about Jesus. Their faith was in Jesus, their life was in Jesus and Jesus' life was in them. And it is this central trust in Jesus that is under threat – and to Paul, if they lose that, they have lost everything.

It wasn't all about Paul; it was all about Jesus. It still is. The letter to the Galatians has something vital to say to us today.

STEPHEN RAND

Dear Galatians

This letter is from Paul, an apostle. I was not appointed by any group of people or any human authority, but by Jesus Christ himself and by God the Father, who raised Jesus from the dead. All the brothers and sisters here join me in sending this letter to the churches of Galatia. May God the Father and our Lord Jesus Christ give you grace and peace. Jesus gave his life for our sins, just as God our Father planned, in order to rescue us from this evil world in which we live. All glory to God forever and ever! Amen.

In our culture, you sign your name at the end of a letter. In Greek culture, you began your letter by stating who you were. Paul gives his name, then uses one word to describe himself – apostle. The Greek word meant emissary – someone sent with a message, a missionary.

And who gave Paul this role? Not a church committee, not even one of Jesus' disciples, but Jesus himself, the living Jesus, raised from the dead by Father God. Paul is insistent that he can write this (angry) letter on the highest authority of all. The implication is that if they reject what Paul has to say, they are rejecting Jesus, rejecting God.

Jesus is the one who gave his life for our sins, in order to rescue us, so Paul is pushing the stakes even higher right at the start of his letter. If you reject me, you are rejecting Jesus; if you reject Jesus, you are rejecting the one who died for your sins and turning your back on the rescue plan of God the Father – and that will leave you back in the evil world, your hope gone.

Paul phrases this in such a way that it seems he is stating a truth about Jesus that his readers will accept. He wants them to join him in saying the 'Amen' at the end of the passage. He wants to establish something they agree with him about before opening up about their disagreement. It's not a bad way to conduct an argument.

What elements of today's world would you consider evil, and in what ways has your faith in Jesus rescued you from them?

STEPHEN RAND

I don't believe it!

I am shocked that you are turning away so soon from God, who called you to himself through the loving mercy of Christ. You are following a different way that pretends to be the Good News but is not the Good News at all. You are being fooled by those who deliberately twist the truth concerning Christ.

Paul wastes no time in getting to the heart of the matter. He has one reason for writing, and his readers would have been left in no doubt just how strongly he felt about it. He's shocked! Other translations of verse 6, such as the NIV and NRSV, say, 'I am astonished'; the KJV has 'marvel', suggesting amazement.

Amazement can be full of admiration or full of incredulity: 'I don't believe it!' Pilate 'marvelled' when Jesus remained silent at his trial (Mark 15:5); his disciples 'marvelled' when Jesus spoke to the Samaritan woman (John 4:27); his listeners 'marvelled' when Jesus instructed them to 'give to Caesar what belongs to Caesar, and give to God what belongs to God' (Matthew 22:21–22). Jesus told Nicodemus not to 'marvel' when he announced, 'You must be born again' (John 3:7).

The Greek word was a standard expression used in Greek letters at this time to indicate incredulity and dissatisfaction. Paul is shocked and amazed. Why? Because the Galatians are being fooled by those who are twisting, perverting and corrupting the good news so that it is no longer good news at all. They are being fooled so much that they are turning away from God.

We live in a time of fake news. Truth has become not only a rare commodity but also one which sometimes seems not to matter much at all. Paul thought that the truth of the good news he had preached and lived was vital and needed to be defended, otherwise those who had received new life in Christ would lose that life and in doing so lose everything.

Paul can't believe the Galatians are throwing away all that they have received through the good news, the truth about Jesus. He is determined that his letter will wave the red flag of danger as strongly as possible.

Father God, help me to know the truth and to defend
the truth with passion, humility and love. Amen

STEPHEN RAND

Direct revelation

Dear brothers and sisters, I want you to understand that the gospel message I preach is not based on mere human reasoning. I received my message from no human source, and no one taught me. Instead, I received it by direct revelation from Jesus Christ... God chose me... It pleased him to reveal his Son to me so that I would proclaim the Good News about Jesus to the Gentiles. When this happened, I did not rush out to consult with any human being... Instead, I went away into Arabia, and later I returned to the city of Damascus. Then three years later I went to Jerusalem to get to know Peter, and I stayed with him for fifteen days. The only other apostle I met at that time was James, the Lord's brother.

To counter the enemies who are twisting the truth, Paul begins by underlining his own credentials. His hope is that, by explaining the basis for his own confidence in the gospel, he will inspire that same confidence in his readers. They know that Paul is a highly educated theologian. They know he is good with words. But Paul does not cite his qualifications or begin with a logical argument. Rather, he reminds them of his life-changing encounter with Jesus on the road to Damascus. The fanatical persecutor of the followers of Jesus met Jesus himself in a blinding blaze of light, and he heard the words, 'I am Jesus, the one you are persecuting!' (Acts 9:5). Jesus identified himself with his followers; Paul's gospel is summarised by the follower's total identification with Jesus.

The Greek words translated 'by direct revelation *from* Jesus Christ' can also be translated 'by direct revelation *of* Jesus Christ': Jesus was both the messenger and the message.

Paul now communicates two important facts using one set of words. He did not receive his message, or adapt it, through any conversations with the other apostles, but he did meet them. The message of Paul, who was chosen by God and given a uniquely personal revelation of Jesus, was not shaped by others, but he was known and accepted in the inner circle.

Jesus, grant me the confidence that comes from knowing you and the assurance of being known by you. Amen

STEPHEN RAND

The gospel to the Gentiles

Then fourteen years later… I met privately with those considered to be leaders of the church and shared with them the message I had been preaching to the Gentiles. I wanted to make sure that we were in agreement, for fear that all my efforts had been wasted and I was running the race for nothing… They supported me and… had nothing to add to what I was preaching… Instead, they saw that God had given me the responsibility of preaching the gospel to the Gentiles, just as he had given Peter the responsibility of preaching to the Jews.

Paul continues to insist that the message he preached, and the authority to preach it, came from God. At the same time he underlines that he had the support and agreement of the leaders of the church in Jerusalem. He does not want his adversaries in Galatia to be able to even begin to suggest that his gospel was different from Peter's and disowned by the apostles in Jerusalem. It would then be all too easy for the twisters of the truth to portray themselves as carriers of the true gospel and Paul as the maverick.

There were not two messages; there were two distinct categories of hearers. From the Jewish perspective the world was divided into two groups: Jews and Gentiles. All the readers of this letter knew that the gospel was rooted in Judaism, that Jesus was a Jew and that all the apostles were Jewish. (My daughter, an RE teacher, tells me that one of her classes was astonished to discover that Jesus was a Jew and not a Christian.)

But the message was not only for Jews. The Greek word translated 'Gentiles' is *ethnos*; it can also be translated 'nations' (ethnic groups). God promised Abraham that 'through your descendants all the nations of the earth will be blessed' (Genesis 22:18); Paul very consciously saw himself as chosen to take forward this commission.

Paul did not invent the idea of Christianity being for the whole world. As a Jew, he knew that this was what God had already planned and promised.

There are probably more Christians in China than any other nation –
all standing in the blessing of the promise to Abraham and
the message of a missionary called Paul!

STEPHEN RAND

Remember the poor

Their only suggestion was that we keep on helping the poor, which I have always been eager to do.

Paul is fighting for the Galatians, desperate for them to hold on to the truth and not be lost. He's been explaining how he met with Jesus, received his message of good news and was given the endorsement of the church leaders in Jerusalem. Then, out of nowhere, he slips in what seems to be an odd aside – they asked me to remember the emergency relief collection.

This collection is referenced elsewhere by Paul, particularly in 2 Corinthians 8—9 (where he says, in what I am sure is not intended as demanding money with menaces, that he will send the brothers round). There was a famine in Jerusalem, and Paul, as he travelled, collected cash that would meet the ongoing needs of the poorest Christians in the church there.

This little aside reveals two things. First, that the division of labour described in yesterday's reading – the gospel for the Gentiles and the gospel for the Jews – was not intended to create two churches, but to build one church in which Jew and Gentile would have concern for one another. And that concern would be expressed practically, in cash. One of the things I loved most about my 25 years with Tearfund was seeing this biblical principle still being expressed and having such an impact – Christians sharing with Christians around the world so that the needs of the poorest could be met.

Second, this verse reminds me that the gospel is good news in every sense: spiritually, physically and practically. You can't receive the good news of Jesus without becoming good news to others. Generosity doesn't make someone a Christian; but a Christian will always be generous. Later in this letter Paul writes, 'Let's not get tired of doing what is good… whenever we have the opportunity, we should do good to everyone – especially to those in the family of faith' (6:9–10).

Loving Father, when things are going well, help me to remember the poor.
And when things are not going so well, help me to remember
the poor. Amen

STEPHEN RAND

Confrontation

But when Peter came to Antioch, I had to oppose him to his face, for what he did was very wrong. When he first arrived, he ate with the Gentile believers, who were not circumcised. But afterward, when some friends of James came, Peter wouldn't eat with the Gentiles anymore. He was afraid of criticism from these people who insisted on the necessity of circumcision… When I saw that they were not following the truth of the gospel message, I said to Peter in front of all the others… 'We know that a person is made right with God by faith in Jesus Christ, not by obeying the law.'

Talk about a clash of the Titans! Paul's conviction and concern are such that he breaks every rule of how Christians should disagree with one another. He confronts Peter face-to-face, in front of everyone; he accuses him of hypocrisy, of leading people astray and of being a coward, afraid to stand up for what he knows is right.

Paul can only behave like this because of what is at stake. It is not just that one could be a Christian without having to become a Jew (by being circumcised) and live like a Jew; it was also that anyone and everyone – whether Jew or Gentile – could only be 'made right with God' on the same basis: 'by faith in Jesus Christ'.

This was not a tactical move by Paul. He was not insisting on this because it would make the gospel more attractive to non-Jews. He was not trying to make Christianity a new religion in its own right rather than a branch of Judaism (though that was a byproduct of his stance). He was underlining what was to him the core truth of the gospel: Jesus is the way, the truth and the life.

And consider this: if Peter could get it wrong and then get it right, so could the Galatians. Their error is not stupid or senseless, and neither is it unforgivable. If Peter can respond positively to Paul's impassioned onslaught, then so can the Galatians. They will be in good company.

Lord, help me to disagree with a fellow Christian only when I am sure it is unavoidable, and always with grace, humility and kindness.

STEPHEN RAND

Crucified with Christ

For when I tried to keep the law, it condemned me. So I died to the law – I stopped trying to meet all its requirements – so that I might live for God. My old self has been crucified with Christ. It is no longer I who live, but Christ lives in me. So I live in this earthly body by trusting in the Son of God, who loved me and gave himself for me. I do not treat the grace of God as meaningless. For if keeping the law could make us right with God, then there was no need for Christ to die.

This is one of those passages that make it very clear that Paul understood what it meant to be a Christian in a way that cuts across not only what many of the Galatians believed but also what many believe today – both inside and outside the church. When he tried to keep the law, he failed; he just couldn't do it. It was impossible to 'meet all its requirements' and so he was condemned. The pass mark in this examination was 100%; anything less was failure. In Romans 3:23, Paul puts it like this: 'Everyone has sinned; we all fall short of God's glorious standard.'

Yet many in our world still believe that if they keep trying to do the right thing, they will earn God's favour, that being a Christian and being put right with God depends on what we do, even when we all know we can't succeed. There's an almost sentimental belief that if I have at least tried, made some effort, that should be enough.

It isn't. If it was, says Paul, why did Jesus die? His answer is almost mystical: because Jesus loved him, Jesus gave himself for him. The death of Jesus brings life to those prepared to die to themselves and live with and for Jesus. Being a Christian means a total willingness to identify with the death of Jesus, to receive the life of Jesus. It's all to do with trust and faith and grace. Jesus puts us right with God.

Jesus loves you and gave himself for you. Look in the mirror,
and say it out loud: Jesus loves me and gave himself for me.

STEPHEN RAND

The real children of Abraham

Oh, foolish Galatians! Who has cast an evil spell on you? For the meaning of Jesus Christ's death was made as clear to you as if you had seen a picture of his death on the cross. Let me ask you this one question: Did you receive the Holy Spirit by obeying the law of Moses? Of course not! You received the Spirit because you believed the message you heard about Christ… In the same way, 'Abraham believed God, and God counted him as righteous because of his faith.' The real children of Abraham, then, are those who put their faith in God.

'Foolish Galatians' was a phrase often used by Greek writers at this time: Galatians were often seen as ignorant barbarians. Paul goes on to say that they have been bewitched. By implication, Paul is saying that by listening to the false teachers they are living up to their stereotypical description; if they want to be wise, they need to believe as they first believed – in the Jesus who died for them on the cross. Paul reminds them of their own experience: they had believed the message about the crucified Christ and had received the Holy Spirit. Obeying the law of Moses had played no part in this process at all.

Mentioning that the law was 'the law of Moses' was a none-too-subtle reminder that the Jews saw themselves as children of Abraham – and Abraham couldn't keep the law of Moses because Moses hadn't yet been born. Abraham was put right with God because of his faith, so the real children of Abraham are those who have faith – those who share his faith, not his ethnicity.

Jesus had made Nicodemus marvel by saying, 'You must be born again' (John 3:7). Nicodemus was incredulous. Every Jew knew that they were born a child of Abraham. That was what made them distinctive, set them apart. But the good news that Paul preached was that by faith in Jesus everyone – Jew and Gentile – could be born again and become a real child of Abraham.

'Father Abraham had many sons; many sons had Father Abraham.
I am one of them and so are you. So let's all praise the Lord!'

STEPHEN RAND

All one in Christ Jesus

For you are all children of God through faith in Christ Jesus. And all who have been united with Christ in baptism have put on Christ, like putting on new clothes. There is no longer Jew or Gentile, slave or free, male and female. For you are all one in Christ Jesus. And now that you belong to Christ, you are the true children of Abraham. You are his heirs, and God's promise to Abraham belongs to you.

Paul insists that everything the false teachers are claiming will be achieved by following the Jewish law is already achieved through faith in Christ. The Galatians, he says, are children of God, with a new relationship that brings access and closeness to the Father. They have been united with Christ, taking on his character as if putting on new clothes. The prodigal son returned home to be greeted by his father saying, 'Bring the finest robe in the house and put it on him' (Luke 15:22). The image of exchanging dirty rags for new clothes is a lovely description of the change that comes from the first discovery of faith in Christ. I remember an elderly woman in Mexico City saying to me, 'For the first time in my life I feel clean.'

Then comes the most world-changing, radical and subversive statement, one that in my view explains why an obscure Jewish sect became a world religion that has transformed the lives, hopes and expectations of millions of people: there is no longer Jew or Gentile – ethnic and racial divisions are broken down; no longer slave or free – social and economic distinctions mean nothing; no longer male and female – men and women share equally in the inheritance that comes from being one in Christ Jesus. The law reinforced these barriers; Jesus removes them.

Genesis 1:27 says, 'God created human beings in his own image… male and female he created them.' Paul is describing a new creation, a new world order. The whole discussion of the law in Galatians has been focused on whether Gentiles needed to be circumcised – an entirely male-only issue. Yes, Jesus is the great liberator of women, and Paul the announcer-in-chief.

How much work is needed for the church to demonstrate that all people, whatever their ethnicity or social class, are one in Christ Jesus?

STEPHEN RAND

Adopted as children and heirs

But when the right time came, God sent his Son, born of a woman, subject to the law. God sent him to buy freedom for us who were slaves to the law, so that he could adopt us as his very own children. And because we are his children, God has sent the Spirit of his Son into our hearts, prompting us to call out, 'Abba, Father.' Now you are no longer a slave but God's own child. And since you are his child, God has made you his heir.

God had a plan – a plan that would fulfil the promises made to Abraham; a plan that would make it possible for individuals to be saved, rescued from the punishment for sin, and reunited and reconciled as children of God, all one in Christ Jesus.

The plan was that, at the right moment, in God's perfect timing, he would send his Son, to be born a Jew and therefore subject to the law, and through his death he would pay the price of freedom, so that those who were slaves could be adopted as children, the children of God.

Paul uses the analogy of adoption, well understood by his readers, to describe the significance of Christ's death on the cross. This was adoption as practised by the Romans; the Jews had no process for adoption. In ancient Rome, when a child was born, the parents could decide to disown the child or to adopt it. Adoption would be a clear sign that the child was chosen by the parents, was wanted, would forever remain one of the family and would not be disowned.

An adopted child received a new identity. All previous commitments, responsibilities and debts were struck off, replaced by new rights and responsibilities. Being adopted made someone an heir to their father, joint-sharers in all his possessions and fully united to him. You can see why Paul thought it a great analogy of what Jesus had done.

And as a member of the family, you had the right to call your father 'Abba'. This was not so much the infant crying 'Daddy', but rather the way a mature adult would address their father.

Father, thank you for adopting me, making me your child and heir.

STEPHEN RAND

Freedom

So Christ has truly set us free. Now make sure that you stay free, and don't get tied up again in slavery to the law. Listen! I, Paul, tell you this: If you are counting on circumcision to make you right with God, then Christ will be of no benefit to you. I'll say it again. If you are trying to find favour with God by being circumcised, you must obey every regulation in the whole law of Moses. For if you are trying to make yourselves right with God by keeping the law, you have been cut off from Christ! You have fallen away from God's grace.

Paul continues to spell out the stark choice facing the Galatians. He insists that they cannot have it both ways. They must choose between following Jesus and no circumcision on the one hand, and being circumcised and therefore abandoning their faith and trust in Christ on the other.

Freedom was a major concept to Paul. He regularly refers to Christ setting people free. Jewish followers of Jesus are set free from the demand to observe Jewish rules and regulations; Gentile followers of Jesus are set free from having to identify as Jews by being circumcised. Both Jews and Gentiles are set free to receive the Spirit of Jesus and to take on the character of Jesus.

Freedom frightens some people. They prefer a set of rules to live by. But freedom can be exhilarating! It is full of life, full of following the guidance of God's Spirit, full of unpredictability, but also full of trust and faith. How tragic that Christianity is seen by so many as an adherence to a set of rules that stifle life. How depressing that churches still create rules, explicit and implicit, that become a barrier to faith and freedom.

The freedom that comes through faith is a gracious gift from God. It comes to us as a free gift; Jesus has paid for it. Imagine it is your birthday, and an enormous parcel is delivered. It is just what you wanted. What would you do? Would you unwrap it and examine it as fast as possible? I doubt you would leave it in the corner unopened, uninterested in what might be inside.

Dear Lord, help me to experience your freedom
and to use it for the benefit of others.

STEPHEN RAND

Fulfil the law: love your neighbour as yourself

For you have been called to live in freedom, my brothers and sisters. But don't use your freedom to satisfy your sinful nature. Instead, use your freedom to serve one another in love. For the whole law can be summed up in this one command: 'Love your neighbour as yourself.' But if you are always biting and devouring one another, watch out! Beware of destroying one another. So I say, let the Holy Spirit guide your lives.

Paul knew he was walking a tightrope. The more he emphasised that those who were 'in Christ' were not required to keep the law and had received the gift of freedom, the greater the risk that his readers would imagine they were free to do whatever they liked, that the moral law no longer applied to them.

To counter this, Paul draws on arguments familiar to those versed in Greek philosophy: freedom within the law was a common theme for discussion. Plato described freedom as a virtue of the soul alongside justice, courage, truth – and self-restraint. Freedom was not seen as an excuse for self-indulgence. Rather, says Paul, freedom must be used to serve one another – not out of duty or legalistic observance, but out of love.

But Paul is not a philosopher; he is quick to refer to Jesus' own teaching, affirming that alongside the command to love God the ethics of the law are summarised in one further command: 'Love your neighbour as yourself.' In fact, this is more than a summary. The Greek word Paul uses is often translated 'fulfil' or 'complete'. If only we could love others, put them first day after day, then the law would have no further demands.

But we can't; no one can – except Christ. That's why we must let his Spirit be our guide. This time the Greek word is literally 'walk'. It implies movement, progression. The freedom we have in Christ is to live and move in the Spirit, a channel for the love of God, not as a slave to the law of God or through pleasing ourselves. Freedom was – and is – not the freedom to live however we want, but the freedom to live as Jesus wants.

Dear Lord, day by day show me how to love and live by your Spirit.

STEPHEN RAND

The fruit of the Spirit

When you follow the desires of your sinful nature, the results are very clear: sexual immorality, impurity, lustful pleasures, idolatry, sorcery, hostility, quarrelling, jealousy, outbursts of anger, selfish ambition, dissension, division, envy, drunkenness, wild parties, and other sins like these. Let me tell you again, as I have before, that anyone living that sort of life will not inherit the Kingdom of God. But the Holy Spirit produces this kind of fruit in our lives: love, joy, peace, patience, kindness, goodness, faithfulness, gentleness, and self-control. There is no law against these things!

These verses spell out the contrast between our sinful nature and the Spirit. Lists of vices and virtues were common in the literature of the time. Paul's list of wickedness is very much a Jewish list of what were seen as Gentile vices. He is very clear ('Let me tell you again') that the gospel is not a licence for any kind of licentiousness or bad behaviour.

It can be alarmingly simple to scan through this list and quickly decide it does not apply to us. We are all, largely, good at making excuses for ourselves. But it is a painful reality that individual lives, families and churches are still being torn apart by sexual immorality, anger, jealousy and more.

Older translations describe the list of vices as the 'acts' or 'works' of the sinful nature. The contrast with the 'fruit' of walking with the Spirit could not be greater. The first list is of specific deeds and actions that damage the individual and society; the second list is of virtues that together describe the qualities of life in the Spirit.

Fruit grows because the plant is rooted in fertile soil, and what could be more fertile than God's life-giving Spirit? The specific virtues that Paul lists are nearly all those that are elsewhere attributed to God. I was brought up on this definition of the work of the Holy Spirit: to make us more like Jesus. When we are 'in Christ', our behaviour will be that of Christ.

Help us to know the joy and peace that are not dependent on our day-to-day situations, but that come from the confidence of your presence whatever our circumstances.

STEPHEN RAND

The new people of God

As for me, may I never boast about anything except the cross of our Lord Jesus Christ. Because of that cross, my interest in this world has been crucified, and the world's interest in me has also died. It doesn't matter whether we have been circumcised or not. What counts is whether we have been transformed into a new creation. May God's peace and mercy be upon all who live by this principle; they are the new people of God.

Paul has poured out his heart for his readers. He has applied his mind to the task of opposing the teaching that threatened to undermine the gospel itself, the good news of what Jesus has done. As he reaches the end of the letter, he spells out the key points once again.

The cross of Jesus has been at the heart of his argument – those who wish to maintain the practice of circumcision as a sign of obedience to the law are in effect denying the validity of Jesus' death for the forgiveness of sin and the resurrection of new life for those who choose to place their faith in Jesus.

Paul sees it in black and white. The 'world' is not a geographical entity, neither the planet nor its people; it is a spiritual entity, all that is opposed to God and what is good. Because Jesus died, Paul is dead to that world and alive in God's kingdom. He is transformed and part of a new creation, one in which circumcision plays no part.

The man who was so determined to preserve Judaism and destroy these Christians now pronounces that the Jewish religion must give way to a new creation inhabited by a new people of God – literally 'the Israel of God'. This phrase – which only occurs here – is still highly contentious 2,000 years later. There are many Christians who remain convinced that the Jewish people are still God's chosen people. In the letter to the Galatians Paul is insistent that faith in the crucified and risen Christ – not ethnicity, not moral behaviour – is the only basis for membership of God's family.

---

*May you – and every member of God's family –
know God's mercy and peace as a daily reality. Amen*

STEPHEN RAND

Holy habits: praying with objects

How do you pray? Most of us will have a preferred style of prayer, often learned in childhood and little altered since. Our prayers can sometimes feel a bit like shopping lists: requests to God, acknowledgement of our failings and perhaps a few thanks for the blessings we've received. This isn't a bad thing, but it can at times become perfunctory – a duty to be carried out before we get on with the day or go to sleep. Yet prayer can be so much more! If we think of God as being like our most trusted friend, someone who knows and understands us, and if we recognise prayer as a way of spending time in God's company, then all sorts of creative possibilities open up.

I'd like to take you on a journey using objects to inspire prayer. The resources required for each day are listed below so that you can prepare in advance the objects you need. Nothing should be difficult to find. A time-table for a two-week period is suggested, but do move between the days if the theme or the activity is not right for you; this is supposed to be an adventure rather than a test! You might not find that all the suggestions feed your prayer life, and that's fine. You may discover that you react better to words or to images, that sound or silence stimulates creativity, or that using your hands helps to guide your thoughts. Above all, trust that God longs to come to you.

Resources:

Week one: Sunday – an apple, a knife and a cutting board; Monday – a photo of someone close to you or an object that brings them to mind; Tuesday – a stone or pebble to hold in your hand; Wednesday – a piece of uplifting music to play, listen to or sing; Thursday – a lump of clay, salt dough or similar modelling material; Friday – a plant cutting, a pot and some potting soil; Saturday – a large sheet of paper and coloured pens.

Week two: Sunday – a recent newspaper; Monday – a notebook; Tuesday – a glossy magazine; Wednesday – two copper coins; Thursday – scented aromatherapy oil; Friday – a cross or crucifix; Saturday – an empty box.

AMANDA BLOOR

Take one apple and eat

So when the woman saw that the tree was good for food, and that it was a delight to the eyes, and that the tree was to be desired to make one wise, she took of its fruit and ate; and she also gave some to her husband, who was with her, and he ate. Then the eyes of both were opened, and they knew that they were naked; and they sewed fig leaves together and made loincloths for themselves.

We don't know what sort of fruit Adam and Eve ate, but it is often portrayed as an apple, so that is what we're going to use today as a focus for prayer. It might seem odd to use the 'forbidden fruit' in this way, but, as a Medieval hymn reminds us, without the apple having been eaten, Christ would not have come to set us free.

Hold an apple in your hand. Feel its weight and the smoothness of its skin, then look at its roundness and the delicacy of its colouring. Satellite imagery shows the earth looking small yet beautiful in the immensity of space; perhaps you can imagine our world – like the apple that you hold – cradled carefully in God's loving hand.

If you cut the apple horizontally into two pieces, you will find that the pips are shaped like a star. Reflect upon the star that heralded Jesus' birth and led worshippers into his presence. Despite humanity's disobedience, God does not turn away, but comes to live among us. Through Christ's self-giving, our failings can be forgiven and our sins redeemed.

Take a moment to inhale the scent of the cut apple, then, finally, allow yourself to take a bite. Slowly and mindfully, taste and eat. Sometimes we rush to satisfy our physical or spiritual hunger without acknowledging the goodness that God has provided. Stop and give thanks.

God of the garden, forgive me for the times I have ignored your guidance. Jesus, who turned the cross into the tree of life, help me to bear good fruit. Spirit of wisdom and truth, fill my emptiness with your presence. Amen.

AMANDA BLOOR

'This is the one'

Jesse made seven of his sons pass before Samuel, and Samuel said to Jesse, 'The Lord has not chosen any of these.' Samuel said to Jesse, 'Are all your sons here?' And he said, 'There remains yet the youngest, but he is keeping the sheep.' And Samuel said to Jesse, 'Send and bring him; for we will not sit down until he comes here.' He sent and brought him in… The Lord said, 'Rise and anoint him; for this is the one.'

We have all had different experiences of family life, and if we have siblings, we might have found that we were expected to conform to a stereotype based upon birth order: the responsible eldest; the indulged youngest; the attention-seeking middle child. In this Bible story, we see Jesse assuming that it must be one of his older children who is called by God, overlooking the qualities of his youngest son, David. God knows each person's potential and never looks past us.

If you have a photograph of the person you wish to hold in prayer today, place this where you can gaze upon it. If you are using an object that represents them, put it in front of you or hold it in your hand. Spend a few moments fixing them in your mind. Think about not just what they look like, but also who they are, how they act and what it is about them that is significant to you. Then close your eyes. Imagine them standing before you, and in your mind's eye take their hand and lead them into God's presence. What would you want to tell God about them? What would you want to ask on their behalf? For what would you give thanks? You can say these things aloud or silently offer them up.

Now put yourself in their place. What might they say to God about you? What might they hope for you? How might they want to offer support? Think about God nodding, listening and smiling. Accept that you are loved and valued too.

Loving God, thank you that I can bring this person to you. Help me to remember that, through your love, they, and I, need never be alone. Amen

AMANDA BLOOR

My rock, my fortress

I love you, O Lord, my strength. The Lord is my rock, my fortress, and my deliverer, my God, my rock in whom I take refuge, my shield, and the horn of my salvation, my stronghold. I call upon the Lord, who is worthy to be praised; so I shall be saved from my enemies... For who is God except the Lord? And who is a rock besides our God?

This psalm is both a prayer and a hymn of praise. David is said to have sung these words to God after being protected from the wrath of King Saul, pouring out his gratitude and giving thanks for deliverance from his enemies. We have all experienced times of difficulty or danger, and we might have cried out for protection and help. Have we also remembered to be grateful for the strength we've found in and through God? Perhaps some of us are struggling at this moment. Prayer can help us to remember that God is strong and steadfast, particularly when we are feeling weak or lost.

Pick up a stone or pebble and hold it in your hand. It might be worn smooth by the action of wind and waves, or it could be rough and jagged with edges as sharp as knives. The stone or pebble you have chosen will reflect both the rock that it came from and the external forces that have shaped or revealed it – a good metaphor, perhaps, for our own lives. Notice how the stone or pebble feels as you pick it up, how it fits into your hand and how it is warmed as you continue to hold it. Look at any colours, patterns and striations. See the beauty in it and remember that it – like you – was created by God.

Now reflect upon the solidity of the rock from which it came. God is our bedrock, our shelter and our hiding place. Offer thanks for that firm foundation beneath our feet and pray for situations where you need God's support.

God, my help and my salvation, let me stand firm upon you.
My fortress and my deliverer, you are my strength. Amen

AMANDA BLOOR

Breaking into song

How beautiful upon the mountains are the feet of the messenger who announces peace, who brings good news, who announces salvation, who says to Zion, 'Your God reigns.' Listen! Your sentinels lift up their voices, together they sing for joy; for in plain sight they see the return of the Lord to Zion. Break forth together into singing, you ruins of Jerusalem; for the Lord has comforted his people, he has redeemed Jerusalem.

Whether or not you consider yourself to be musical, it's deeply instinctive to react to music. We sing lullabies to soothe babies to sleep, we tap our feet to a catchy beat and in church we raise our voices to God in hymns of praise and thanksgiving. Isaiah describes how a people, long oppressed and enslaved, will literally sing for joy when God sets them free. Their hearts will be so full that they won't be able to remain silent.

Singing with words brings together emotion and intellect, and we might find that singing about our faith, or singing parts of the liturgy, helps us to memorise texts or to find deeper meaning. But singing can also, as the Bible passage reminds us, be a simple expression of delight. If you've ever hummed a tune as you've gone about the tasks of the day, you'll know that there's often no need for words; the music says all that is necessary.

Today, let music be your prayer of thanksgiving. If you play an instrument, then choose a piece of music that you can offer to God. If you sing, then lift your voice, making sure that if you use words, they say what is on your heart. Even if you think yourself unmusical, try making a joyful noise – God won't judge your skills! Perhaps you would prefer to listen to a favourite piece of music instead. Let your soul be uplifted and your heart filled with joy.

Generous God, from whom all good gifts come,
thank you for the gift of music. Fill me with joy, that
I may lift up my voice and always sing your praise. Amen

AMANDA BLOOR

The potter and the clay

The word that came to Jeremiah from the Lord: 'Come, go down to the potter's house, and there I will let you hear my words.' So I went down to the potter's house, and there he was working at his wheel. The vessel he was making of clay was spoiled in the potter's hand, and he reworked it into another vessel, as seemed good to him. Then the word of the Lord came to me: Can I not do with you, O house of Israel, just as this potter has done?

We each know how we deal with changing circumstances or unexpected difficulties. We might be phlegmatic in the face of disaster or we might panic at the slightest setback. Some of us will relish a challenge, while others like a quiet life. Yet life is unpredictable and the future unknown. Jeremiah felt inadequate when called to be a prophet, but he learned to trust God and speak words of wisdom to his people. Their future looked bleak and many felt abandoned by God, yet Jeremiah saw, in the actions of the potter, a deeper truth.

If we are spiritually or mentally fragile, it's easy to feel like the vessel in this passage, spoiled and crumpled up – worthless. But if we allow God into our lives, we can be gently drawn into a new form, as a skilled potter shapes clay. God can make us something beautiful.

Take a piece of clay, salt dough or modelling material and roll it around in your hands. Feel how malleable it becomes, how pressure changes its shape and how the lightest touch of your fingers leaves impressions. Reflect upon your life. What has shaped you? What were the moments that left their mark? Now squash down the clay before shaping it into an open vessel. See how the shape is affected by the material itself as well as by your hands. If this pot or bowl symbolised your life, how would you ask God to continue shaping you? And with what would you wish to be filled?

Shape me, O Lord, into something that seems good to you.
Whenever I feel spoiled, build me up. Rework me with love. Amen

AMANDA BLOOR

Transplanting and growth

Thus says the Lord God: I myself will take a sprig from the lofty top of a cedar; I will set it out. I will break off a tender one from the topmost of its young twigs; I myself will plant it on a high and lofty mountain… in order that it may produce boughs and bear fruit, and become a noble cedar. Under it every kind of bird will live; in the shade of its branches will nest winged creatures of every kind.

The creation story began in a garden, and in this passage from Ezekiel we are given an image of God as gardener. The language used throughout the book draws a sharp contrast between the power of God and the weakness of humanity, yet God, though disappointed at the people's sins, wants to bring about a better future. If they are ashamed of their iniquities and return to the Lord, the covenant will stand.

It is God who created the world and all that is in it; it is God who brings about the conditions for growth. Breaking off a tender shoot from the top of the tallest tree, God plants it so that it can put down roots, grow branches and produce fruit. Birds will find shelter in it, and it will be described as 'noble'. New growth will outstrip the old.

Take a cutting from a suitable plant and place it into a pot of damp soil. Keep it somewhere warm and light and water it regularly, and you should soon see signs of growth. As you prepare the cutting, ask God to help you look at your life. What needs to be cleared away so that new growth can sprout? Are you drawing your energies from the living water that is Christ, or are your roots shallow and congested? Are you planted in the right place, or would you thrive in a different situation? Trust that God, the gardener, can help you to bear good fruit.

Great God, I give my life into your careful hands. Make of me what you will. I am a tender twig; help me to grow strong and tall, that I may offer shelter to those in need. Amen

AMANDA BLOOR

Counting the generations

An account of the genealogy of Jesus the Messiah, the son of David, the son of Abraham. Abraham was the father of Isaac, and Isaac the father of Jacob, and Jacob the father of Judah and his brothers... So all the generations from Abraham to David are fourteen generations; and from David to the deportation to Babylon, fourteen generations; and from the deportation to Babylon to the Messiah, fourteen generations.

My father spent many years visiting libraries and record offices before drawing up a family tree. In these days of electronic information, there seems to have been a resurgence of interest in genealogy. What is it, I wonder, that we hope to find when we investigate our ancestry? As television programmes have shown, looking at the past can throw up surprises, but often it's the more trivial details that fascinate. We seem to share a need to recognise who we are by understanding where we've come from.

The gospel of Matthew begins with ancestry. This is who Jesus is, it tells us: the Messiah linked with Solomon, David, Isaac and Abraham. This is how he fits into Jewish family – and salvation – history. The irony is that Joseph is Jesus' stepfather, so Jesus has no biological links with these great figures. Yet they are his family and they matter.

It can be instructive to draw a map of how we fit into our own networks. Take a large sheet of paper and write your name in the middle. Add the names of those who are significant to you now: friends, a partner, children, colleagues. Use different colours to differentiate relationships and symbols to show affection, conflict or brokenness. Go backwards and add in figures from the past, then look ahead and think about the future. You might wish for children or grandchildren or have hopes for the people you love. Add them in. Now ask God to help you look clearly at the page. See how you are part of a much larger whole. Ask for healing of hurts and for blessings upon all.

God, who called me to life, help me to remember that I am part of your family, linked with others, all loved by you.

AMANDA BLOOR

Good news

There was a man sent from God, whose name was John. He came as a witness to testify to the light, so that all might believe through him. He himself was not the light, but he came to testify to the light. The true light, which enlightens everyone, was coming into the world... John testified to him and cried out, 'This was he of whom I said, "He who comes after me ranks ahead of me because he was before me."'

I recently spent a night in Dartmoor under a simple lean-to shelter. The night was clear and cold, and the view of stars across a truly dark sky, without any light pollution, will stay with me. Yet moving about was difficult and felt dangerous; I stumbled my way over rough ground, afraid to fall and starting at every sound. We are so used to having light at the flick of a switch and walking along well-illuminated pavements that we can forget how challenging it can be to navigate in the darkness.

John the Baptist knew that he lived in a time when darkness had held sway for too long. Yet he looked through the shadows for glimmers of hope. He drew attention to Christ, the 'true light' that was entering the world, and he became a messenger of the wonderful news of God's grace. A faithful witness to what he had seen, John spoke truth and spread hope. He prepared the way of the Lord so that others could truly see.

All too often, the news we hear or read seems bad. There are tragedies, salacious gossip, criticisms and fears. But there are good things, too, if we look for them. Today, take a newspaper and look carefully through it. If your eye is caught by unhappy news, then pray for those people or situations, but read on. Find some positive stories and give thanks to God for them. Let your heart be lifted.

Glorious God, you brought us the best news of all: the birth of our Saviour, Jesus Christ. Help us to be bearers of joyful news, encouraging one another and trusting in your goodness. Let us point others to Christ's light. Amen

AMANDA BLOOR

Seeking wisdom

When the festival was ended and [Mary and Joseph] started to return, the boy Jesus stayed behind in Jerusalem, but his parents did not know it... When they did not find him, they returned to Jerusalem to search for him. After three days they found him in the temple, sitting among the teachers, listening to them and asking them questions. And all who heard him were amazed at his understanding and his answers.

There are different types of knowledge. In this passage, the young Jesus, anxious to learn more about his faith and his God, stays behind in the temple, engaging with the teachers there. He's a bright boy, impressing those who hear him, but he might not have realised that Mary and Joseph would be frantic with worry when they couldn't find him and that they would likely be critical of his thoughtlessness towards his parents. That's another lesson to learn.

I wonder how you would describe yourself to a stranger who asked questions about your own knowledge or wisdom. Some of us might have been good students, with qualifications to demonstrate our academic success. Some might have practical gifts and are good with our hands, able to build and to mend. Some are creative, seeing beauty in the world, and some have the emotional maturity and sensitivity to support people in difficulty or need. All sorts of knowledge are valuable; none are better than others. What a dull world it would be if we all had identical skills and gifts!

Use a notebook to record the different types of knowledge, wisdom, insight and action that you come across this week, in yourself and others. You might want to write things down, draw pictures or create a scrapbook. Pray, as you do this, that you may see where God is in all this. What can I offer to God through the gifts that I have been given? And how do I recognise God in other people?

Dear God, you created me and gave me unique gifts and skills. Help me to value the types of knowledge I see in others and in myself. May I offer them back to you and to your world. Amen

AMANDA BLOOR

Worship and temptation

Then Jesus was led up by the Spirit into the wilderness to be tempted by the devil… The devil took him to a very high mountain and showed him all the kingdoms of the world and their splendour; and he said to him, 'All these I will give you, if you will fall down and worship me.' Jesus said to him, 'Away with you, Satan! for it is written, "Worship the Lord your God, and serve only him."'

Jesus was tempted when he was vulnerable. Each time the devil tried to entrap him, Jesus turned back to God. Life is more than food, he insisted; God is not to be tested; the things of this world are nothing. It is God only who deserves worship and service.

We know this, but we also know that temptation is hard. In this age of media celebrity and conspicuous consumption, it's easy to forget where freedom is to be found. A new item of clothing, the latest gadget or a heavily promoted experience is likely to give only transient satisfaction, while famous figures can reflect an unrealistic picture of body image or lifestyle. Of course, it's fine to have an occasional treat. Life is to be enjoyed! But when longing for something becomes an obsession, it's dangerously close to worship. And worship belongs only to God.

Spend some time looking at a glossy magazine. Ask Jesus to help you to see clearly. What is it that attracts? What do you desire? And what does that say about you? If we long to be like another person, we might be unhappy with our current situation. If we are dreaming of owning the new shoes or the expensive watch, we might be feeling overlooked or unimportant. If we are considering going into debt to go on holiday, we might be running away from the mundane or the challenging. Let Jesus reassure you. These things are false idols and will not bring satisfaction. You are loved and valued as you are. Worship only the Lord your God. Be set free.

Jesus, my Saviour and my friend, walk with me when I feel rejected or insignificant. Help me not to desire worldly things, but to turn instead to God. Amen

AMANDA BLOOR

Value and cost

He looked up and saw rich people putting their gifts into the treasury; he also saw a poor widow put in two small copper coins. He said, 'Truly I tell you, this poor widow has put in more than all of them; for all of them have contributed out of their abundance, but she out of her poverty has put in all she had to live on.' When some were speaking about the temple, how it was adorned with beautiful stones and gifts dedicated to God, he said... 'The days will come when not one stone will be left upon another.'

Oscar Wilde described a character who knew the price of everything and the value of nothing. Jesus might have smiled at that comment. Look at the contrasts in the passage above: the widow's tiny coins set against the precious gifts given by wealthy donors. The widow quietly gives all that she has, while the rich give what is showy and obvious. Her offering will outlast the more visible 'beautiful stones and gifts dedicated to God'; the temple will fall, but her generosity will be treasured by God.

Sometimes we can overlook little things in favour of showier gestures. It's easy to measure ourselves against others and feel inadequate or to think that God wants only the biggest and best. When we feel that we have little to offer, we are probably closer to God than when we believe that we have done something wonderful.

Place two copper coins in front of you. They are worth little on their own, and many people don't bother to save them. But they were made with care; look at their design, feel their solidity and measure their weight. Think of a small thing that you could do for God today. Offer it in prayer. Imagine how large the store of coins would be if there was one for each day of your life, and how that store would grow if added to the similar offerings of other Christians. Ask God to help you see the value, rather than the cost.

Generous God, help me to offer all that I am,
however small that may seem to be. Accept my gift. Amen

AMANDA BLOOR

Kindness and care

Mary took a pound of costly perfume made of pure nard, anointed Jesus' feet, and wiped them with her hair. The house was filled with the fragrance of the perfume. But Judas Iscariot, one of his disciples (the one who was about to betray him), said, 'Why was this perfume not sold for three hundred denarii and the money given to the poor?'… Jesus said, 'Leave her alone. She bought it so that she might keep it for the day of my burial.'

Mary must have known what it felt like to be exhausted and afraid. Jesus was at a formal dinner given by Lazarus and his sisters. They meant well, but being the guest of honour at a large function is not a relaxing experience. His disciples asked questions, a large crowd gathered outside and Martha acted as hostess. Then Mary broke through all the conventions of polite behaviour in order to respond to the need she recognised in Christ. She opened a container of costly ointment, massaged it into his tired feet and wiped it away with her hair. It was at once a gently caring and startlingly intimate act, made all the more resonant by the powerful perfume that lingered in the air. Judas grumbled, but Jesus defended Mary's actions. 'Leave her alone,' he warned. 'She understands.'

Although Mary's use of the oil was extravagant, it was not a display of wealth. Instead, it was a recognition of the needs of the moment. What value would there be in waiting until after death?

As Mary cared for Christ, so God cares for you. Take some scented aromatherapy oil and warm it in your hands. Inhale deeply, acknowledging its scent. Then massage it into your hands and your forearms, discovering any tension or aches there, and knead them away. Be aware of the issues that concern you. Let God into the most troublesome parts of your life, with a gentle touch that shows kindness and love. Pray for the support you need.

Touch my life, loving God, with the care I need today. Give me the strength to show that care to others, through Jesus Christ, our Lord. Amen

AMANDA BLOOR

Names, titles and identities

So they took Jesus; and carrying the cross by himself, he went out to what is called The Place of the Skull, which in Hebrew is called Golgotha. There they crucified him, and with him two others, one on either side, with Jesus between them. Pilate also had an inscription written and put on the cross. It read, 'Jesus of Nazareth, the King of the Jews.' Many of the Jews read this inscription.

John's gospel describes the crucifixion in bleakly sparse language. Jesus is taken from Pilate's headquarters and carries his cross to Golgotha, where he is crucified between two others, whose names or crimes we do not know. All that matters is Jesus, the central character in this horrific drama.

When Jesus is first taken to Pilate, he is asked if he is a king and replies, 'You say that I am.' The Roman soldiers call him 'King of the Jews' as they torment him, and the chief priests who demand his execution claim that they have no king other than the emperor. For them, the anonymous title 'king' is identity enough and the name of the man they disdain so much is irrelevant.

Yet when Pilate has Jesus crucified, he orders a sign erected on the cross. At this moment of ultimate pain and indignity, both name and identity are brought together. This is Jesus of Nazareth, the King of the Jews. It is a statement of uneasy respect.

Gaze prayerfully upon a cross or crucifix, and reflect upon the inscription placed over Christ's head. Consider each of its elements. *Jesus*: the name given by an angel, spoken lovingly by Mary and Joseph, called out by his friends, denied by Peter. Speak that name. *Of Nazareth*: the place that was home, that shaped the child into the man, that was apparent in his accent, that was dismissed by a critic as insignificant. Remember that good came out of Nazareth. *King of the Jews*: a title that Jesus never claimed, that only hinted at his true power and authority. Give him glory and honour.

Jesus of Nazareth, King of the Jews, God with us, help me to see beyond names and titles and love you as you are. Amen

AMANDA BLOOR

He has risen

But on the first day of the week, at early dawn, they came to the tomb, taking the spices that they had prepared. They found the stone rolled away from the tomb, but when they went in, they did not find the body. While they were perplexed about this, suddenly two men in dazzling clothes… said to them, 'Why do you look for the living among the dead? He is not here, but has risen.'

I'm sure I'm not the only person who can't resist popping into unfamiliar churches or cathedrals when I'm travelling. It's fascinating to look at the architecture, read memorial tablets and admire stained glass. Some buildings seem to hum with holiness, while others can seem disappointingly flat. It's nothing to do with beauty, although that can be a bonus; some of the most spiritual places I've visited have been simple and undistinguished.

There is a danger, however, that we can expect to find God only in the 'right' sort of places. As Jesus' friends discovered on that first Easter morning, the resurrection puts paid to any notion that the divine can be confined. Expecting to tend Christ's broken body, they instead are faced with an open doorway, discarded linen and an empty tomb. 'He is not here,' say angels. 'He has risen.'

Take an empty box and, with God's help, picture all the things that you have buried deep: painful experiences, unhappy memories, injustices, regrets. In your imagination, place them in the box and close the lid. Now pray that God will take those things and put them to death. They have no more power to hurt or destroy. Spend some time accepting this. Then open the box and look upon the emptiness there. Ask God to fill the emptiness with love. Let that love flow outwards, filling your heart and life, moving onwards through you into the world. Say to yourself, 'He has risen.' All things, with God's help, can be redeemed. All, with God's help, is possible.

Jesus, my Saviour, you overcame death and rose to new life.
Help me to rise above the things that I need to put to death in my life.
Help me to believe. Amen

AMANDA BLOOR

The book of Ruth

'Story' is said to be the natural language of the brain. From the beginning of time, story has been used as a brilliant vehicle for communicating truth. For instance, just think of the pithy, memorable parables our Lord Jesus told. The heart-warming book of Ruth gives us one of the most complete and uplifting stories in the Old Testament. Even though it is a comparatively slim book, Ruth's story is crammed with truth, both theological and social. It portrays the truth of God's loving providence and the truth that the witness of a faithful believer has power to change lives.

Ruth is both easy to read and relevant for today's reader. We don't have to be scholars to warm to this riches-to-rags-to-riches account from another age and culture. Four chapters are not difficult to read in one go, and you may find this a helpful exercise to do before starting these daily notes. The author is tantalisingly anonymous, and the book has been squeezed between the fierce book of Judges and the lengthy narratives found in the two books of Samuel.

As we journey together over these next 14 days, let's ask some searching questions of this story. What was considered so important about the book of Ruth that it became included in the Old Testament canon? Did Jesus learn about and love this story? What contemporary themes confront and challenge us, some 3,000 years later?

As we read the account, we see how the lives of two women, Ruth and her mother-in-law Naomi, are inextricably linked. Is this a prompt for us to look at our own lives and recognise the influence, support and love given to us by family or friends? It is also a vivid reminder that complex issues in Ruth's time have their contemporary counterparts: the ravages of famine, disease, bereavement, racial discrimination, infertility, the treatment of strangers, mixed marriages and the human spirit for survival.

Jesus commended the widow's mite above the rich people's offerings (Mark 12:41–44). The story of the widow Ruth begins in poverty and grief but shines through all time with loyalty, trust and love.

ELIZABETH RUNDLE

Hopes and dreams in tatters

In the days when the judges ruled, there was a famine in the land. So a man from Bethlehem in Judah, together with his wife and two sons, went to live for a while in the country of Moab… Now Elimelek, Naomi's husband, died, and she was left with her two sons. They married Moabite women, one named Orpah and the other Ruth. After they had lived there about ten years, both Mahlon and Kilion also died, and Naomi was left without her two sons and her husband.

For the early listeners to this story, people who professed rather than obeyed Yahweh, the covenant God of Israel, this first verse would have brought a sharp intake of breath. Moab! Why on earth would Elimelek take his family to Moab? To get a feel for the hostility Moab aroused, we need to pause and glimpse the backstory.

Within received memory, the Israelites had been conquered by the Moabites and endured 18 years of humiliation (Judges 3:12–14). Their plight was seen as God's punishment for their disobedience to God's laws. All in all, there remained common animosity towards Moab. In Elimelek's defence, however, the land of Moab was visible across the Jordan rift valley from his own land in Bethlehem. Did he see streaks of fertile green where fresh springs watered crops in the shadow of the barren hills? We are given the merest details from which to build the picture of a desperate family, fleeing from devastating famine while they still had strength. You get the idea that Elimelek would have gone to the moon to save his wife and sons.

How tragically topical is the plight of hungry people. Whether displaced by famine, floods, earthquakes or conflict, innocent human suffering touches our hearts.

We don't know if Kilion and Mahlon accepted the Moabite gods along with their Moabite wives, but we do know that Naomi remained faithful to the God of Abraham, Isaac and Jacob. Despite the tragedy that had befallen them, all their crushed hopes and dreams, Naomi continued her trust in the Lord her God.

Lord, give me strength and faith to carry on
when hopes disintegrate around me.

ELIZABETH RUNDLE

Integration and mixed marriage

The leaders came to me [Ezra] and said, 'The people of Israel, including the priests and the Levites, have not kept themselves separate from the neighbouring peoples with their detestable practices, like those of the Canaanites, Hittites, Perizzites, Jebusites, Ammonites, Moabites, Egyptians and Amorites. They have taken some of their daughters as wives for themselves and their sons, and have mingled the holy race with the peoples around them...' When I heard this, I tore my tunic and cloak, pulled hair from my head and beard and sat down appalled.

From the standpoint of countries in the so-called developed world, Ezra's attitude is jarring. But this is where we take our leap across time to build up our understanding of Elimelek's family. God's great servant Moses had led slaves out from under Egyptian oppression and, over many years, evolved their identity as God's people. Laws laid down by Moses were to keep God's people pure and separate from the gods of surrounding peoples. Separation led to mutual distrust and hostility. There is an irony here, in that alongside the laws of morality and purity given by Moses is the statement: 'God is God of gods... who shows no partiality' (Deuteronomy 10:17). This was the grand theory – but grand theories and human nature seldom stay together.

Picture this immigrant family with their basic and immediate need for food, water and shelter. How were they received in Moab? It seems they met with a degree of tolerance that might not have been shown had the roles been reversed. In Ruth 1:3, we read that Elimelek dies. Does this underline his poor physical state on arrival in the new country? Whatever the initial circumstances, widowed Naomi and her sons not only remain in the foreign country, but both sons take Moabite wives. The story is developing.

Here we see the power of love that overcomes expectations and convention. It is indeed a reflection of almighty God's all-embracing love for humanity, his creation. Love is the major theme throughout the Bible, brought to fulfilment in the life and teaching of Jesus.

Help me, Lord, to show tolerance and compassion to those who, today, seek food, shelter and love in a foreign land.

ELIZABETH RUNDLE

Bereavement

When Naomi heard in Moab that the Lord had come to the aid of his people by providing food for them, she and her daughters-in-law prepared to return home from there. With her two daughters-in-law she left the place where she had been living and set out on the road that would take them back to the land of Judah.

In Old Testament times there were three types of widows: those left with nothing, those with sons and those with no sons but with land inherited through their deceased husband. Living in a foreign land, bereft of husband and sons, Naomi was in a perilous position. How would she survive? Any widow reading this will understand the raw and aching emptiness of Naomi's grief. However, we live in times which emphasise 'support systems'. What support could Orpah and Ruth expect, having married men from Bethlehem? Would Moabite men consider them less-than-suitable wives?

We have all seen the physical toll of grief on people, and Naomi was no different. The years and triple bereavement had drained and shrunk her. Perhaps you too have blamed God for the death of a loved one. Although Naomi accused God of making her life bitter, she, like Job, did not turn away from God. Naomi's was not a fair-weather faith; whatever happened she had the confidence to be honest with God.

Into this dire situation shines a faint gleam of hope. When we delve back into the laws and rights of antiquity, we realise that Naomi was entitled to Elimelek's land in Bethlehem, but only if she (impossible) or a daughter-in-law bore a son, who could continue Elimelek's line and redeem the land. The brightest ray of hope lay in news from Bethlehem. The famine was over! Naomi did not wallow in the past; she grasped the possibility of future security for herself and her daughters-in-law back in Bethlehem.

Death and destitution are never a thing of the past; we don't have to look far to find Naomis, Ruths and Orpahs. Yet alongside these human heartbreaks is the overarching guidance and providence of the eternal, loving God. For Naomi, a woman with deep faith, God's providence was her beacon of hope.

Lord, I pray for simple trust like Naomi's.

ELIZABETH RUNDLE

Choices

Then Naomi said to her two daughters-in-law, 'Go back, each of you, to your mother's home. May the Lord show you kindness, as you have shown kindness to your dead husbands and to me. May the Lord grant that each of you will find rest in the home of another husband.' Then she kissed them goodbye and they wept aloud and said to her, 'We will go back with you to your people.' But Naomi said, 'Return home, my daughters. Why would you come with me?'

Three women had set out with high expectations until, suddenly, Naomi was overcome with misgivings. What kind of life could she offer her Moabite daughters-in-law, Orpah and Ruth? Why would they stay with her? We are looking at life-changing choices here.

Because the book bears the title of Ruth, it's easy to overlook the remarkable strength of character and example of Naomi. She would have had no choice in her husband's decision to make a future beyond Bethlehem, and, as a widow, she had no choice other than to return to Bethlehem. It was a different matter for the two younger women. Their obvious choice would seem to have been to stay within their natural family community and start again with Moabite husbands. However, both chose to go with Naomi and leave their natural families. Why? What a warm and encouraging friend they found in Naomi, but more than that, Naomi's steadfast faith through adversity was an example they wanted to be near.

Orpah's heart chose Naomi, but her head chose the safe option with familiar surroundings and opportunities (1:14). Have you made a choice you have later regretted? Regret is a crippling emotion, yet we all harbour it. While Naomi had no choice but to return to Bethlehem, Orpah's choice was to stay at home. Ruth, on the other hand, chose to step out in faith.

Maybe you have choices to make today or in the near future. Take your choices to God and pray for his guidance: God knows and understands.

'Guide me, O thou great Redeemer… I am weak, but thou art mighty; hold me with thy powerful hand' (William Williams, 1717–91).

ELIZABETH RUNDLE

Leaving all behind

But Ruth replied, 'Don't urge me to leave you or to turn back from you. Where you go I will go, and where you stay I will stay. Your people will be my people and your God my God... May the Lord deal with me, be it ever so severely, if even death separates you and me.' When Naomi realised that Ruth was determined to go with her, she stopped urging her. So the two women went on until they came to Bethlehem.

Yesterday we thought about choices; today is all about the implications and consequences of life-changing choices. We could say that Orpah played it safe, while Naomi decided on the only realistic course of action open to her. Ruth's choices were monumental. Not only was she embarking on a new life in a foreign country, but she also chose to embrace a new god, the God introduced to her by Elimelek's family, especially Naomi.

In whatever century, changing religion is never undertaken lightly and not accomplished in isolation. Each religion comes with its own rituals, traditions and group identity. Ruth was prepared to leave behind everything she had ever known. That was what leaving home meant in those days. Some have likened this courage to the conviction of the first missionaries who crossed to unknown worlds with the gospel message. Naomi's glowing faith made such an impact that her widowed daughter-in-law responded with loving support.

It is our response to the teaching of Jesus that marks us as followers of Jesus Christ. Reading about him, hearing about him and thinking about him do not commit us into a trusting relationship of faithful service. Our relationships with other people will always mirror our response to God in Jesus. The gospel is lived out by actions every bit as much as by words.

Take a few moments to recall how you felt when you left home. Were you in a different country needing to learn a new language and customs? Did you find a group of Christians for support? Remind yourself of the people who brought the love of God into your life when it was most needed. Ask yourself who needs your encouragement today.

'Through the love of God our Saviour, all will be well'
(Mary Bowley Peters, 1813–56).

ELIZABETH RUNDLE

Role-reversal

So Naomi returned from Moab accompanied by Ruth the Moabite, her daughter-in-law, arriving in Bethlehem as the barley harvest was beginning… And Ruth the Moabite said to Naomi, 'Let me go to the fields and pick up the leftover grain behind anyone in whose eyes I find favour'… So Boaz said to Ruth… 'Stay here with the women who work for me. Watch the field where the men are harvesting, and follow along after the women.'

Millions of refugees in the world today struggle with life- and role-reversal. But it is also a situation that at any time, through reasons of finance, health or age, any one of us could experience. Naomi had left Bethlehem in the protection of her husband; she returned older and suffering from triple bereavement, the same woman, yet altered by circumstances beyond her control. Ruth, the once-happy bride, was reduced to the uncertain prospects of a migrant worker. The roles of these two women were reversed by tragedy.

Biblical authors had the gift of imparting a whole picture with the fewest brushstrokes. In just a few words, the reader is left in no doubt about Naomi and Ruth's plight. Although in reduced circumstances, Naomi remained the matriarch from whom Ruth needed permission to do things. The very mention of leftovers gives a stark illustration of the depth of their poverty. They were next door to beggars. In Leviticus 19:9–10 we find provision laid down in the law of Moses specifically for such needs. This was God-inspired social altruism. Ruth's last few words to Naomi here hold the poignant recognition that, as a foreign woman, she would not be safe in everyone's fields. What a stain on civilisation that the same is true today.

In those times barley and wheat were sown in the autumn, with barley, the staple of the poor, ripening first. Women who followed the harvesters to glean were followed by Ruth. In her changed role Ruth showed that she was not afraid of hard work in her responsibility for her mother-in-law.

'Through all the changing scenes of life, in trouble or in joy,
the praises of my God and king, my heart and tongue employ'
(Nicholas Brady and Nahum Tate, 1696).

ELIZABETH RUNDLE

101

Faithfulness in all things

Boaz replied, 'I've been told all about what you have done for your mother-in-law since the death of your husband – how you left your father and mother and your homeland and came to live with a people you did not know before. May the Lord repay you for what you have done. May you be richly rewarded by the Lord, the God of Israel, under whose wings you have come to take refuge.'

For those like me who have lived in a village or small town, we know how fast news – or gossip – spreads. The fact that a Moabite woman had come to Bethlehem would have been red-hot news. Today, let us step aside from the ancient story to the essential truth behind the book of Ruth.

Although the book follows in the wake of the stories of the patriarchs, the great Moses, Joshua and Israel's judges, we find no charismatic hero here. Nor are there any momentous battle victories or challenging rules for personal and corporate living. Ruth could be considered an inconsequential little love story that does nothing to further our understanding of the almighty God. That assumption could not be more wrong. The book of Ruth is a testimony to the loving kindness of our creator God. It reflects God's faithfulness towards both nation and individual and, in particular, brings into focus the important role of the redeemer, the restorer or deliverer (in Hebrew, *goel*). These terms enable us to understand more clearly the role of our Lord Jesus, who came into our world to offer redemption and salvation to those who believe in him. Jesus is our *goel*.

Much like the parable of the good Samaritan, in which Jesus shocked his hearers by using a Samaritan as the source of compassion, this book would have been shocking to many. Ruth, the foreigner – and worse, a Moabite – is the example of loyalty and loving kindness. It highlights the disparity between the scriptures, the word of God, and the actions of his people, so easily led down paths of bigotry and prejudice. Those particular paths are wide and eagerly followed.

'The fruit of the Spirit is love, joy, peace, forbearance, kindness, goodness, faithfulness, gentleness and self-control' (Galatians 5:22–23). Gracious God, may this fruit be my aim and desire.

ELIZABETH RUNDLE

Generous attitude

Boaz gave orders to his men, 'Let her gather among the sheaves and don't reprimand her. Even pull out some stalks for her from the bundles and leave them for her to pick up, and don't rebuke her.' So Ruth gleaned in the field until evening. Then she threshed the barley she had gathered, and it amounted to about an ephah. She carried it back to town, and her mother-in-law saw how much she had gathered. Ruth also brought out and gave her what she had left over after she had eaten enough.

Ruth was a hard worker. After her long day she had a long climb up the steep hill into Bethlehem town. Boaz showed generosity by telling Ruth she could share the precious drinking water, inviting her to eat with the harvesters and giving instruction to the men not to harm her. In other words, Boaz gave her protection and sustenance. None of scripture is incidental, and the author was drawing on the parallel between Boaz's treatment of vulnerable Ruth and the protection and provision which the almighty God gave his people. This would have been written within firm memory of God's provision for the wandering Hebrew slaves, following Moses in the desert. God had provided, and God would provide.

Ruth responded to this generosity with her own generosity towards her mother-in-law, Naomi. Likewise, Naomi had not put any pressure on the younger woman to stay with her when she had determined to return to Bethlehem – quite the reverse; her attitude, to both Orpah and Ruth, had been selfless. Real love is not possessive, offering guidance but not restraints, always considering the other person's welfare. Ruth even gave Naomi what was left over from her own lunch. In this context, 'left over' does not have the connotation of 'I didn't want it so you can have it'; rather, Ruth's thoughts went to Naomi's need, and she willingly shared her meagre treat of roasted grain.

All our actions bring about reactions, responses and consequences. What a change we could make within families, communities and countries if all our actions were motivated by generosity and love.

Generous God, you have blessed me with the gift of this day.
Help me respond with generosity towards the vulnerable.

ELIZABETH RUNDLE

The First Sunday of Advent   103

'The Lord bless him!'

Then Ruth told her mother-in-law about the one at whose place she had been working. 'The name of the man I worked with today is Boaz,' she said. 'The Lord bless him!' Naomi said to her daughter-in-law. 'He has not stopped showing his kindness to the living and the dead.' She added, 'That man is our close relative; he is one of our guardian-redeemers'... So Ruth stayed close to the women of Boaz to glean until the barley and wheat harvests were finished.

I don't believe anyone's heart is full of praise and thanksgiving in every moment of their life. The Bible reassures us that even icons of faith wrestle with their doubts and disappointments. The great prophet Elijah was overcome by suicidal depression (1 Kings 19:4), and Jesus wept at Lazarus' death. Naomi's faith in the almighty God took a severe knock as bereavement hit her three times. As was the common idea at the time, Naomi attributed her plight to God: 'The Almighty has brought misfortune upon me' (Ruth 1:21). She stated what she saw as fact without resentment or recrimination.

But though Naomi was down, she was definitely not out. Her reaction to Boaz affirms that her heart-warming faith, which had so influenced Ruth, was restored. It is where we share a tiny point of contact with this faithful widow, for how often do you hear the words 'Bless you' in gratitude to someone's kindness today?

Without doubt Naomi was helped back in Bethlehem by others who trusted in Israel's God. It helps us all to have the company of those whose faith we share and, in difficult times, to receive their prayerful support. The way Boaz addressed his workers and adhered to the law to provide for the widow and the alien (Leviticus 23:22) shows he was a kind, God-fearing man. A reminder of the blessing given by God to Abraham (Genesis 12:3b), Naomi had found a guardian-redeemer, a possible saviour to lift herself and Ruth from their poverty. The God of Israel would provide for them and also provide a future to keep Ruth's dead husband's name alive.

In your quiet time today, give thanks to God
for the person who has been a blessing to you.

ELIZABETH RUNDLE

Finding a home

Naomi said to her, 'My daughter, I must find a home for you, where you will be well provided for. Now Boaz… is a relative of ours. Tonight he will be winnowing barley on the threshing-floor. Wash, put on perfume, and get dressed in your best clothes. Then go down to the threshing-floor, but don't let him know you are there until he has finished eating and drinking. When he lies down, note the place where he is lying. Then go and uncover his feet and lie down. He will tell you what to do.'

Looking at these four verses we need to lay aside our preconceptions about marriage. This is almost impossible, bombarded as we are with wedding fairs, bridal-wear shops and the mounting paraphernalia surrounding wedding preparations, clothes, venues and exotic honeymoons. In those faraway times, marriage was the means to further the mutual benefits of peace and prosperity.

So let's return to Ruth, a destitute widow in a foreign country. Because there was no father to secure a fruitful union, Naomi took that responsibility on herself. She turns to the tradition, laid down by Moses in Deuteronomy 25:5–10, to pursue what is known as the levirate. This was the custom that enabled a dead man's widow to marry the nearest relation, so that a son born of the new union would carry the dead man's name and inheritance. It was a shrewd method of keeping the family group together without losing possessions and land. Naomi's sons would have inherited Elimelek's land in Bethlehem, but with neither husband nor sons to provide, Naomi looked to Boaz for security by marrying Ruth.

As far removed as we are from biblical times, basic preparations for a bride remain the same. Today it may be a spa treatment, aromatic oils and a new wardrobe; Ruth, in the manner of her day, prepared for marriage. Boaz was the man who could redeem her. She and Naomi would be safe; they would not go hungry; they would have a future (see Jeremiah 29:11).

The idea is carried forward through the centuries. Jesus, our redeemer, said: 'Whoever comes to me will never go hungry, and whoever believes in me will never be thirsty' (John 6:35).

Lord, give me tolerance and empathy with a stranger's plight.

ELIZABETH RUNDLE

Waiting

[Boaz said,] 'And now, my daughter, don't be afraid. I will do for you all you ask… Although it is true that I am a guardian-redeemer of our family, there is another who is more closely related than I. Stay here for the night, and in the morning if he wants to do his duty as your guardian-redeemer, good… But if he is not willing, as surely as the Lord lives I will do it. Lie here until morning.'

Just as the future looked secure with the man Ruth had learned to trust, Boaz defers to a closer relative. With everything up in the air, the tension grew. Ruth and Naomi had to wait. Waiting involves patience and that, for most of us, is guaranteed to fray the nerves. Have you ever been waiting on a result that changed your life? This was precisely the knife-edge situation in which Ruth found herself. Having offered herself to Boaz, not knowing made her even more vulnerable. And so we glimpse the village politics – the way that ten elders of the community would sit and deliberate a matter at the city gates, the precursor to councils, committees and parliaments.

Boaz comes across as a sensitive relative and honourable citizen. I find it interesting that this closer relative had, so far, kept out of the picture. But, just in time, the unnamed guardian-redeemer appeared (4:1). Boaz kept to the letter of the law regarding Elimelek's lands which the closest guardian-redeemer was willing to accept (Leviticus 25:25–28). However, the thought of taking a Moabite widow was a step too far. He most likely had one wife, and possibly more, and a son by Ruth would return the land from his family to Ruth's. It was complicated but a valid reason for relinquishing his claim as primary guardian-redeemer (Ruth 4:6). Boaz could take the land and Ruth.

Contrary to the rebuff from the closest relative, the elders appeared delighted to witness Boaz's success and, regardless of Ruth's Moabite heritage, which had been repeatedly mentioned, gave the couple their fulsome blessing (4:11–12). How remarkable that they linked Ruth, the outsider, to the venerated wives of Jacob – Rachel and Leah!

Thank you, Lord, for people who have reached out to help me
at pivotal times.

ELIZABETH RUNDLE

Reflecting God's generosity

[Boaz] also said, 'Bring me the shawl you are wearing and hold it out.' When she did so, he poured into it six measures of barley and placed the bundle on her. Then he went back to town. When Ruth came to her mother-in-law, Naomi asked, 'How did it go, my daughter?' Then she told her everything Boaz had done for her and added, 'He gave me these six measures of barley, saying, "Don't go back to your mother-in-law empty-handed."'

The book of Ruth is small, but crammed with detail. These past two weeks, we have followed the storyline, concentrating on specific verses. Today, let's broaden our approach. The Bible contains 66 books, but there is a consistent theme to them all: the almighty God's power and love, together with God's abiding care for the individual as well as the nation.

In today's verses we are told of Boaz's generosity beyond the cultural observance of providing for the poor. This act of kindness reflected God's generosity – the one, true God of Israel, their redeemer and sustainer. The people retained the memory of manna and quail in the desert (Exodus 16:4–13), which saved them from starvation. This continued thought process is most beautifully portrayed in the Psalms. The ritual chanting of the Psalms embedded the character of God in their minds, so that it was natural to look to God for protection, provision, restoration and salvation rolled into one.

Fast-forward into the New Testament to find our Lord Jesus feeding 5,000 people (Luke 9:12–17) and even more dramatically saying, 'I am the bread of life. Whoever comes to me will never go hungry' (John 6:35). The way Boaz generously gave the measures of barley is not to be seen as payment for Ruth's night at the threshing floor, but an acknowledgement of her dependence and added responsibility for Naomi. As a God-fearing man, the barley was a pledge of his good intention.

In what ways can we be generous to the vulnerable today?

Meditate on these words: 'God's grace was so powerfully at work in them all that there was no needy person among them' (Acts 4:33–34).

ELIZABETH RUNDLE

'Better to you than seven sons'

So Boaz took Ruth and she became his wife. When he made love to her, the Lord enabled her to conceive, and she gave birth to a son. The women said to Naomi: 'Praise be to the Lord, who this day has not left you without a guardian-redeemer. May he become famous throughout Israel! He will renew your life and sustain you in your old age. For your daughter-in-law, who loves you and who is better to you than seven sons, has given him birth.' Then Naomi took the child in her arms and cared for him. The women living there said, 'Naomi has a son!' And they named him Obed. He was the father of Jesse, the father of David.

It's strange to think of friends, people of our immediate community, having the honour of naming our child. But, look again: neither Ruth nor Boaz named their son. The women's prayer, or blessing, over the child rang with tenderness and special praise for Ruth. In a culture where the sons bore the future hope, 'better to you than seven sons' was the highest praise.

Obed, whose name meant 'servant', would indeed become famous. His name may not immediately jump to our minds, but, as grandfather to the iconic King David, Obed would certainly have been known throughout Israel. Obed was part of a Bethlehem dynasty from which Israel's second king would come, and also our Lord Jesus.

As our thoughts on the book of Ruth come towards a close, we think of Bethlehem, the town associated with Naomi, Ruth and Boaz, King David and Jesus. The prophet Micah's inspired messianic prophecy, 'Out of you will come for me one who will be ruler over Israel' (Micah 5:2), elevated this small town for all time. Bethlehem, 'house of bread', was destined to become the birthplace for God's Messiah, 'the bread of life' (John 6:35). What irony that Elimelek, Naomi, Mahlon and Kilion were driven from Bethlehem through devastating famine.

Today, the Church of the Nativity in Bethlehem, possibly the oldest church in the world, is a UNESCO Heritage site.

Thank you, Lord, for the millions of pilgrims drawn to Bethlehem.
Through the loving kindness and steadfast faith within the book of Ruth,
draw me close to your living presence.

ELIZABETH RUNDLE

Inclusive Bethlehem

This is the genealogy of Jesus the Messiah the son of David, the son of Abraham… Salmon the father of Boaz, whose mother was Rahab, Boaz the father of Obed, whose mother was Ruth, Obed the father of Jesse, and Jesse the father of King David.

In a couple of weeks the global spotlight will turn towards Bethlehem. Words from Luke's gospel will ring out through churches, schools and halls: 'So Joseph also went up from the town of Nazareth in Galilee to Judea, to Bethlehem the town of David, because he belonged to the house and line of David' (Luke 2:4). Young voices will read the story of Jesus' birth for the first time, while older voices recall once more the mystery and miracle of the incarnation.

However, to the early listeners to this story, or readers of the written word, who expected purity of nationhood, there lurked a shocking fact. So important was the family line for the biblical writers that the genealogy of Jesus is recorded in both Matthew's gospel (Matthew 1:1–16) and Luke's (a reverse version, Luke 3:23–38). Notice that in Matthew, four women are named within the list: Tamar, Rahab, Ruth and Mary. Ruth, the *Moabite*! Surely this points to the all-inclusive love of God, to whom obedience, faithfulness and compassion are the hallmarks of his people before ethnicity or gender. God is not confined by religious bureaucracy.

Ruth is the eighth book of the Old Testament. In Hebrew the number seven represented the perfect number, while eight signified new beginnings. Let's digest these meaningful symbols. In Ruth 4, the word *goel* (redeemer) is used a dozen times. Redemption was key in the physical life of Naomi and Ruth. Today, redemption is key in our spiritual lives.

This Christmas, the modern city of Bethlehem will be thronging with Christians from all over the world. Manger Square will be packed with worshippers celebrating the greatest miracle of all – the birth of a Saviour, our Saviour. Pipe bands, drums and choirs will proclaim 'Christ is born in Bethlehem'. Jesus Christ, God's Son, was born into our human world to redeem us, restore us and be our *goel*.

Glory to God in the highest – and on earth, peace.

ELIZABETH RUNDLE

A Celtic Advent

For 'In him we live and move and have our being'; as even some of your own poets have said.
ACTS 17:28

Over the next couple of weeks we will be journeying through a part of Advent with the Celtic saints. Celtic Christianity is influencing a lot of people in the modern church, and one of the reasons for this might be that they discern something a little different from the traditional way of seeing things. This, for many, is bringing refreshment to their spiritual lives.

You will notice that throughout my reflections I often use the term 'Divine' rather than 'God'. This is not something one particularly finds in Celtic Christianity; rather it is from my own journey. I find that the word 'God' often has a lot of baggage for many, and that people are far too easily misled to the idea of a masculine deity when the word 'God' is used. So I more often use the term 'the Divine' when referring to the Christian deity – the whole Trinity, as the more traditional word 'God' generally means. This is why I also use a capital 'D' rather than a lower-case one, in the same way that people would write 'God' rather than 'god' when referring to the Christian deity. I have found that this is much more inclusive to folk who have struggled with the church 'God' or who have a different spiritual perspective or belief altogether.

In the same way, my prayers, rather than beginning with 'Father God' or 'Dear Lord', might begin in a more open way, similar to the manner used by Nan Merrill in her book *Psalms for Praying* (Continuum, 2007). I hope that by my slightly different semantics you find something 'more' in these devotions.

Great Divine, open my heart and mind…

DAVID COLE

Beginning our preparations

And whatever you do, in word or deed, do everything in the name of the Lord Jesus, giving thanks to God the Father through him.

I am a frequent visitor to the Holy Island of Lindisfarne. It is one of my favourite places in the UK. I have been every year since the early 2000s, and these days I go multiple times a year to lead retreats in The Open Gate, the Community of Aidan and Hilda's retreat centre on the island.

Anyone who has been there will tell of the special feeling it has. It is what one might term a 'thin place', where the veil between the physical world and the spiritual/supernatural world feels thin. For many centuries the island has had Christians praying around it, drawing down the divine presence, which might account for that feeling.

These days it is pilgrims and retreatants, but in times past it was monks. The first people to ever set up any settlement on the island were a group of monks in the seventh century who had travelled from Iona, with Aidan as their bishop. Before they did anything, however – before they started their ministry, before they built the monastic centre – they spent 40 days prayer-walking the island, spiritually preparing the place and themselves for what was to follow. This practice of stopping for a period of prayer before stepping into action seems to be the usual practice for the Celtic saints. Numerous tales are told of a 40-day prayer vigil before an activity. Celtic Advent was also 40 days.

In all our preparations leading up to Christmas, with so much to do, do we ever stop to spend time quietly in prayer? Not just our daily Bible reading (like you are doing now), but a time of stillness and quiet – just 'being' with God. Do we even see the importance of involving God, right from the beginning, in everything we do? Perhaps you do it with the important things, but is it done in 'whatever you do', as it says in today's passage from Colossians?

Loving One, before I begin any task, great or small,
remind me to pause to focus upon you,
to draw you into what I am doing.
Lead and guide me in everything.

DAVID COLE

Songs of innocence

And Mary said, 'My soul magnifies the Lord, and my spirit rejoices in God my Saviour, for he has looked with favour on the lowliness of his servant. Surely, from now on all generations will call me blessed; for the Mighty One has done great things for me, and holy is his name. His mercy is for those who fear him from generation to generation. He has shown strength with his arm; he has scattered the proud in the thoughts of their hearts. He has brought down the powerful from their thrones, and lifted up the lowly; he has filled the hungry with good things, and sent the rich away empty. He has helped his servant Israel, in remembrance of his mercy, according to the promise he made to our ancestors, to Abraham and to his descendants forever.'

Most years my family and I will go to some outdoor Christmas carol event. Quite often these are Victorian themed, because the Victorians were the greatest lovers of Christmas (perhaps). We love to join in with the songs. It is part of our Christmas tradition.

Singing carols is something which brings joy to our hearts. I know that singing in general at any time of year can do that, but there is something different, something particularly special, about Christmas carols, or just Christmas songs, which raises our spirits.

In the Celtic culture, pre- and post-Christianisation, songs and folk tales were a huge part of life. Communities would gather in the evenings and on feast days to tell tales and sing songs together. The nativity story was one of those tales that would have been sung about. We may not know exactly what Christmas carols the Celtic monastic centres were filled with, but we can be sure that they would have been singing with gusto the story of the birth of Christ.

However, the trouble with singing the same songs every year is that we can often lose sight of the depth and meaning of the words. As you sing Christmas carols this year, look at the words with fresh eyes. See the lyrics, and raise your voice in praise!

Holy One, I praise you! (Add your own personal praise.)

DAVID COLE

Mary's angelic visitation

And [the angel Gabriel] came to her and said, 'Greetings, favoured one! The Lord is with you.' But she was much perplexed by his words and pondered what sort of greeting this might be. The angel said to her, 'Do not be afraid, Mary, for you have found favour with God. And now, you will conceive in your womb and bear a son, and you will name him Jesus...' Then Mary said, 'Here am I, the servant of the Lord; let it be with me according to your word.' Then the angel departed from her.

I have never seen an angel with my eyes in the supernatural sense (although I know those who have), but I'm convinced that I have seen them in physical form (Hebrews 13:2), and I have definitely felt their presence, which feels different to the divine presence.

Angels for the Celtic saints were as everyday as any other aspect of their faith. We have many stories of angelic encounters from the lives of the saints. Some saints, such as Columba, were particularly well known for their time spent with angels, and even in commanding angels – see the chapter on Columba in my book *Celtic Saints* (BRF, 2020). For the Celtic Christians, angels were around to protect them and help them in the dangers of life, and they had prayers for this, especially directed towards Michael, the warrior archangel. Angels also served as messengers of God.

For Mary in today's passage, for Joseph later in the nativity story and for the Celtic saints, as for many other saints through the ages, angelic encounters changed the course of their lives. These beings brought messages from God which changed everything, sometimes in minor ways and sometimes in major transitions.

Mary saw a figure standing before her; Joseph was spoken to in a dream. How open are you to receiving divine guidance, and then obeying it, through supernatural encounters such as angelic visitations?

DAVID COLE

The Word made flesh

He is the image of the invisible God, the firstborn of all creation... For in him all the fullness of God was pleased to dwell.

It has been known for me to slip out of everyday clothes and don some slightly augmented Victorian-style garb. The reason for this is to attend steampunk gatherings, which I find rather fun! Steampunk is a subculture based upon Victorian science fiction, particularly expressed by writers such as Jules Verne and H.G. Wells. Within these gatherings, attendees are transformed from their everyday selves into something completely different. Some people go as far as having steampunk names, usually preceded by an aristocratic title. My musician friend Jack, for example, becomes Duke Box.

This idea of taking off one form of self and putting on another one, beautifully expressed through the steampunk scene, is at a much deeper level what happened at the incarnation of the Cosmic Christ. And, perhaps equally as important, it is what can happen to us because of the incarnation of the Cosmic Christ.

The ninth-century Irish theologian John Scotus Eriugena said: 'He who from God made himself a human being, makes gods from human beings. [Scripture says] "and dwelt among us" – that is, possessed our nature so as to make us participants in his nature' (Christopher Bamford, *The Voice of the Eagle*, Lindisfarne Books, 2001). In other words, Christ took off his divine glory and put on humanity so that we might transcend our humanity to put on his divine nature (see 2 Peter 1:4).

Although Jesus was fully divine and fully human simultaneously – the great paradox, as Pierre Teilhard de Chardin calls it – he 'emptied himself... being born in human likeness. And being found in human form' (Philippians 2:6–7). He took off the divine glory that was his in the heavenly realms and took on flesh. The Divine took on human nature so humanity could take on the divine nature.

How do we respond to that? How do we allow the Divine to transform us into the divine nature?

---

*Jesus Christ, Son of the Father, help me to allow you
to transform me to become more like you.*

DAVID COLE

Cobblers

But whoever obeys his word, truly in this person the love of God has reached perfection. By this we may be sure that we are in him: whoever says, 'I abide in him,' ought to walk just as he walked.

I belong to a dispersed Celtic new monastic community. My expression within the community is known as a 'monastic voyager'. 'Voyager' is what we call those who have taken vows into the community, but I have decided to live out our way of life (our Rule) a little more strictly and more traditionally monastic. This includes wearing a habit. This has been a part of the community's vision since it began over 25 years ago, but I was the first to formulate it into a lived-out practice. Part of this formulation was to research the psychology of clothing, and how what we wear can change the way we behave from a subconscious level.

Our behaviour is such an important part of who we are both as human beings and as followers of Christ. Pelagius, a British monk who lived in the fourth and fifth centuries, said that we should 'not flatter ourselves merely on possessing the name and being called Christians… No one is assigned any name whatever without due cause: to be called a cobbler, it is necessary to produce shoes; it is his skill in his craft which causes a man to be called an artificer or craftsman… for it is by examples of this kind that we recognise that there is no name without an act… How can you then be called Christian, if there is no Christian act in you?… He is a Christian who is one not only in name, but in deed, who imitates and follows Christ in everything' (B.R. Rees, *Pelagius*, Boydell Press, 2004).

Living out what we say we believe is as important as what we believe in the first place. This is not an opportunity for guilt at how bad we might be at representing Christ, but an opportunity to reflect on how much we allow the Divine to transform us to become better reflections of divine glory.

Perfecter of life, may my actions reflect my beliefs.

DAVID COLE

Breastplates

I pray that, according to the riches of his glory, he may grant that you may be strengthened in your inner being with power through his Spirit, and that Christ may dwell in your hearts through faith, as you are being rooted and grounded in love.

At our front door, as you step on to our doorstep, you will find a number of things: a large stone with a Celtic knotwork tree of life painted on it (by my wife) with our house name on it; a plaque with a blessing on it for guests; a wooden mezuzah with the Shema in it; and a tile with part of St Patrick's breastplate prayer spiralled on it.

Divine and angelic protection isn't something you hear a great deal about in the modern church. Perhaps we don't feel the need for it so much these days. (*Really?*) But for the Celtic Christians, it was a normal part of life. Two specific types of protection prayer can be found in Celtic Christianity: the Caim, which means encircling and which drew on passages such as Psalm 34:7; and the Lorica, or breastplate. This latter type usually included in its concept of protection the sense that Christ was in us and around us, with the inclusion of phrases such as 'Christ in me; Christ with me; Christ within me; Christ above me, to my left and to my right'.

The fact that Christ is with us and within us, surrounding us and infilling us, is significantly important to every Christian. But how often do we really think about it? How often do we really contemplate what it means to have Christ with us and within us and what that means for our everyday life? How often do we include any such statement in our prayers to reaffirm to ourselves that this reality is where we live?

Why not memorise the simple words of today's prayer? These words, which are on the tile at our front door, are taken from an ancient Celtic breastplate prayer. Use them as a constant reminder of the reality in which you live each and every day.

Christ with me; Christ before me; Christ behind me; Christ within me.

DAVID COLE

Nature

God's angry displeasure erupts as acts of human mistrust and wrong-doing and lying accumulate, as people try to put a shroud over truth. But the basic reality of God is plain enough. Open your eyes and there it is! By taking a long and thoughtful look at what God has created, people have always been able to see what their eyes as such can't see: eternal power, for instance, and the mystery of his divine being.

I'm privileged to live at the edge of the 152 square miles of national parkland known as the New Forest, on the south coast of England. Each day I take my dog out for a walk among its tall trees and sweeping heathland. The sense of the divine presence in such a place is almost tangible. Without a great deal of effort, you can easily become deeply aware of God at your fingertips.

God loves the world – the whole of creation, not just humans, and he interacts with it. But more than that, God is in every part of the natural world. We can encounter the divine in nature, because nature is saturated with the divine.

This was something deeply interwoven in the Celtic Christian mindset. One of the earliest recorded catechisms in Celtic monasticism comes from the fourth-century St Ninian, who founded Whithorn. A young monk asked Abbot Ninian about knowing the will of God. Ninian told him to study. 'And what is the fruit, the conclusion of this study?' the young monk asked. Ninian's reply is deeply moving: 'To perceive the eternal word of God reflected in every plant and insect, every bird and animal, and every man and woman.'

Great Creator of all, teach me to see you in all things and all people, that I may treat all with the same love and respect that I show you.

DAVID COLE

Rules and ways

'Go therefore and make disciples of all nations, baptising them in the name of the Father and of the Son and of the Holy Spirit, and teaching them to obey everything that I have commanded you. And remember, I am with you always, to the end of the age.'

A friend of mine runs numerous marathons each year to raise awareness and money for breast cancer research. She began this when she was in her own remission. When she started, she was an 'ordinary' mum who walked to the school to collect her children and around the village in general. She was no great athlete. However, she decided that she would be dedicated to this venture, so had to set out quite a fitness regime to progress from an everyday level of fitness to the level of being able to run multiple marathons a year. There was no getting away from the fact that the greater dedication she gave to her fitness regime and the more self-discipline she had, the fitter she became.

So often physical realities can be used as analogies of our spiritual reality, and this is no exception. Discipline has always been a part of relationship with God, to progress from the ego-filled, self-centred person, which the apostle Paul describes as the 'old self', to the 'new' (or original) self, which he says we are being transformed into. Discipleship includes discipline, and setting out a way of life (a term I prefer to 'regime', which I use for the physical disciplines) is one of the ways to do this.

In the fourth century there was a British Christian teacher who said that we make so many decisions in a single day that we cannot possibly weigh up the consequences of each. Therefore, he said, to have a Rule (a way of life) is one way in which we can ensure that we are more often going to remain on the right path in our walk with God. To be a disciple is to stick to spiritual disciplines. What are yours?

Gracious One, guide me along the right way; teach me the benefits of a disciplined life, that I will grow more deeply in you. Amen

DAVID COLE

Holy lives

Whoever says, 'I abide in [Christ]', ought to walk just as he walked.

Occasionally someone crosses our life path who seems to emanate, to radiate, the divine character, the very essence of Christ. They seem to embody a depth of peace and holiness that the average person just does not seem to possess. I do not think these people are a special kind of person with some kind of esoteric connection to God beyond the reach of 'normal' people. They have simply spent so much time in the divine presence and allowed it to work in them that Christlikeness simply seeps out of them as they live their everyday lives.

Perhaps someone you know or once met fits this description. We often desire to simply be in their presence. This really is what it means to be 'Christ-ian' – being prepared in this life for the return of Christ by becoming like him, living like Christ. In his *Ecclesiastical History of the English People*, Bede's portrayal of Aidan of Lindisfarne gives the impression that Aidan was one such person who overtly emanated and radiated the very essence of Christ.

We can very easily admire these types of people but feel that we could never be anything like them. This is simply not so. We can all achieve this same sense of embodiment of the divine, of Christlike qualities. We simply need to allow the Spirit to work in us and transform us, and then live fully from that.

Holy and Awesome One, may I let go of my inner self and allow you to fully transform me, that I would embody a Christlike character in an authentic and real way. May your presence within me affect those around me, simply by you being in me and I being with them. Amen

DAVID COLE

Soul friends

Iron sharpens iron, and one person sharpens the wits of another.

Life can be a difficult path to negotiate. Sometimes we may struggle or just need a bit of guidance. The wonderful reality is that we don't have to do this alone. In fact, we are designed to have others alongside us to help us (Genesis 2:18). I have a friend with whom I have a close relationship, and together we walk along life's path, sharing a great deal about what is happening. There is a deep sense of trust, openness and vulnerability that enables a depth of truth and authenticity to be a part of our walk. As we are both fans of J.R.R. Tolkien's Middle Earth adventures, my friend, slightly tongue in cheek, calls me the wizard, saying our relationship is a bit like Gandalf and Bilbo in *The Hobbit* or Frodo in *The Lord of the Rings*, or even like Merlin and Arthur in the legends. In the ancient Celtic culture, and therefore something that flowed into Celtic Christianity, this kind of relationship was called an '*anam cara/chara*' – literally translated 'soul friend': the presence of another person as a companion along the path of life to give advice and guidance as we walk.

The 20th-century Catholic mystic John O'Donohue, in his book *Anam Cara: Spiritual wisdom from the Celtic world*, says, 'Human presence is a creative and turbulent sacrament, a visible sign of invisible grace... Friendship is the sweet grace which liberates us to approach, recognize and inhabit this adventure [of life]... The *anam cara* was a person to whom you could reveal the hidden intimacies of your life. This friendship was an act of recognition and belonging.' Such was the importance of this relationship within Celtic Christianity in Ireland that there arose the expression, 'A person without a soul friend is like a body without a head.'

We don't always like to be vulnerable with others, but from my own personal experience a carefully chosen other can be like fresh air in a stale room or the warm sun shining on our face in the cold winter.

---

*Do you have a soul friend? If not, consider finding
someone you could walk life's path with.*

DAVID COLE

The greatest gift

'For God so loved the world that he gave his only Son, so that everyone who believes in him may not perish but may have eternal life.'

One of the best parts of Christmas for me is watching my children opening their presents. Although I do love and appreciate the gifts I receive, there is nothing quite like watching them unwrap theirs, especially when it is something they really want but aren't expecting. The look of surprise and joy is immeasurable.

One year there was a particular thing my daughter wanted: a figure from Terry Pratchett's 'Discworld' books. We visited the only official merchandise shop in the summer, and she saw the advert for it, which said it was 'coming out soon'. I said that I would keep an eye out and perhaps she would get it for Christmas. No one said anything about it again until about two days before Christmas, when she came with wide, sad eyes and reminded me what I had said. I looked at her, reflected her wide, sad eyes and said, 'Oh yes, we said we would try to get it for you for Christmas, didn't we?'

She went away with her shoulders slumped. What she didn't know was that I had indeed kept in touch with the shop, and it was already wrapped along with the rest of her presents. When Christmas morning came and she and her little brother began unwrapping their presents, I watched as she picked up this figure. She looked at it, a little confused. I got my camera ready. As she unwrapped it, the biggest smile and greatest expression of joy burst out of her! It didn't matter what else she received, that surprise present was the best thing she was given that year, and it still holds a prominent place in her life and bedroom.

Of all wonderful gifts, however, the gift we remember most at this time is, of course, the gift of the Christ.

Generous Father, thank you for giving your Son.
Jesus, thank you for giving yourself.
Holy Spirit, thank you for giving the means for the Christ to live within us.

DAVID COLE

The Festival of Nine Lessons

For many of us in the UK, and other countries where it is broadcast, Christmas begins with the first haunting note of a solo chorister singing 'Once in royal David's city' at the start of the Festival of Nine Lessons and Carols in King's College Chapel, Cambridge, on 24 December. For me and my family it is especially significant since we celebrate on Christmas Eve, in the Austrian style I was brought up in. The service has been held in Cambridge since 1918, but it originates from Truro Cathedral as early as 1880. Through Bible readings and carefully chosen traditional and modern carols, it retells the story of salvation from the fall in the garden of Eden to the incarnation of God in Christ and the promise of God's kingdom.

This series of notes explores the set readings for the Festival of Nine Lessons, with occasional reference to carols and poems. As a great lover of Christmas, and also one who likes to look at the big picture of the Bible's overarching story, I have found writing them stimulating and encouraging. These readings implicitly tell us that God has a plan for all creation, in which the effects of individual and social sin are reversed in a new creation, ushered in by God's presence on earth in Jesus. They approach salvation not as a process of rescuing individuals out of this world, but rather as a total transformation of this world, beginning with the transformation of individuals who are placed in a kingdom community. As a result, they open our eyes to a wider understanding of scripture and a commitment to caring for God's world.

These are also some of the first scriptures I encountered. As a child I heard them every year in English and German, in the beautiful Anglo-German carol service at Coventry Cathedral, which my parents attended and for which my father sometimes played the piano. In a candlelit setting, with a focus on reconciliation which started after World War II (when the original cathedral was destroyed), they planted in my mind seeds of a faith in the one who came to us in Jesus, whom we celebrate at Christmas. I hope they may inspire you too.

VERONICA ZUNDEL

Bad news, good news

The Lord God said to the serpent, 'Because you have done this, cursed are you among all animals and among all wild creatures; upon your belly you shall go, and dust you shall eat all the days of your life. I will put enmity between you and the woman, and between your offspring and hers; he will strike your head, and you will strike his heel'… And to the man he said, 'Because you have listened to the voice of your wife, and have eaten of the tree about which I commanded you, "You shall not eat of it," cursed is the ground because of you; in toil you shall eat of it all the days of your life… you shall eat bread until you return to the ground, for out of it you were taken; you are dust, and to dust you shall return.'

The story of 'salvation history' in the Nine Lessons and Carols starts (as evangelism sometimes has to) with the bad news. Because of human sin, creation and its relationship with humans – who are meant to be its guardians – have gone awry. This is most evident in the judgement on Adam, but also in that on Eve, not included in the verses quoted above: one of her greatest gifts, the ability to bear children, will become a source of pain and suffering. Note, however, that only the serpent and the ground are cursed; there is no curse on the human beings, who are merely told the consequences of their actions.

My own slant on the story of the fall is that the serpent (representing the devil, who as we know from scripture is a liar) offers Adam and Eve something they already have but do not realise it. Made in the image of God, they are already 'like God' and need no further knowledge. The ironic result is that they become less like God, because they now know what it is to sin.

The good news is that in Christ we are being restored into the full image of God, and this is available to all. What helps you to become more Christlike?

In a climate crisis, this reading is particularly poignant.
What can you do to combat climate change?

VERONICA ZUNDEL

Losing and gaining

The angel of the Lord called to Abraham a second time from heaven, and said, 'By myself I have sworn, says the Lord: Because you have done this, and have not withheld your son, your only son, I will indeed bless you, and I will make your offspring as numerous as the stars of heaven and as the sand that is on the seashore. And your offspring shall possess the gate of their enemies, and by your offspring shall all the nations of the earth gain blessing for themselves, because you have obeyed my voice.'

As the mother of an only child, whom I had at an advanced age after fertility problems, I find the story of Abraham's willingness to sacrifice Isaac disturbing and puzzling, as I'm sure many of us do. In its context, it is an ancient and mysterious tale which may have been influenced in some way by the writer's surrounding culture. Why would God give Abraham and Sarah the legitimate child they longed for, after years of waiting, only to take him away again?

Yet there is a sense in which all parents have to give their children back to God. As my father said in his speech at my wedding (written by my mother) you do not own your children; they are only entrusted to you. And that was hard for him to say, as my parents lost their only son at 27. The same is true not only of children but of all God has given us: talents, achievements, possessions. Anything, or all, may be lost at any time. But as Abraham found, God is a specialist in giving back to us what we thought we had lost.

In the context of the Nine Lessons, this reading foreshadows the gift of God's own Son, who would indeed be sacrificed at the hands of human cruelty. We should not think of this as God remaining aloof while his Son was killed; rather, 'in Christ God was reconciling the world to himself' (2 Corinthians 5:19) – God suffered in Christ.

---

*Christ died, not only to atone for sin, but also so that
we will forever know God understands our sufferings.*

VERONICA ZUNDEL

From darkness to light

The people who walked in darkness have seen a great light; those who lived in a land of deep darkness – on them light has shined… For a child has been born for us, a son given to us; authority rests upon his shoulders; and he is named Wonderful Counsellor, Mighty God, Everlasting Father, Prince of Peace. His authority shall grow continually, and there shall be endless peace for the throne of David and his kingdom. He will establish and uphold it with justice and with righteousness from this time onwards and forevermore. The zeal of the Lord of hosts will do this.

If you are familiar with Handel's *Messiah*, you will probably be singing after reading this! These beautiful poetic words are as packed with promises as a Christmas pudding is with dried fruit.

As a Mennonite by conviction, my mind focuses immediately on the promises here regarding peace. Often we think of peace as something Jesus will bring when he returns, something only possible in an ideal world. But the kingdom of God began when Jesus appeared on earth for the first time, and it is continually growing through the action of God's Spirit in us. So peace is something we can work towards now, whether in a small way in our families, workplaces or local communities, or at a national or international level through our votes and campaigning. How will we get to an ideal world unless we practise our ideals?

Yesterday I heard a preacher say that faith is not 'a leap in the dark'. My immediate thought was, 'No, it's a walk in the light.' When we begin our journey of faith, we may have our eyes only half-open, rather like the man healed from blindness who saw people 'like trees, walking' (see Mark 8:22–25). But as we live for Christ, though there will be periods that feel as if fog has descended, the overall direction is one of growing light.

The word 'zeal' in the last verse is interesting. We tend to associate this word with narrow fanaticism. But what if we translated it as 'passion'? We all want to be passionate about our calling – and God is passionate about creating a new world.

VERONICA ZUNDEL

125

A new creation

The wolf shall live with the lamb, the leopard shall lie down with the kid, the calf and the lion and the fatling together, and a little child shall lead them. The cow and the bear shall graze, their young shall lie down together; and the lion shall eat straw like the ox. The nursing child shall play over the hole of the asp, and the weaned child shall put its hand on the adder's den. They will not hurt or destroy on all my holy mountain; for the earth will be full of the knowledge of the Lord as the waters cover the sea.

This isn't often remarked on, but the original creation as described in Genesis 1 and 2 was entirely vegan: 'God said, "See, I have given you every plant yielding seed that is upon the face of all the earth, and every tree with seed in its fruit; you shall have them for food"' (Genesis 1:29). It was a far cry from what Tennyson described in his poetry as 'nature, red in tooth and claw'. Instead of predators and prey, with enmity between different species and all creatures exploited by humanity, the Bible portrays a world of community and peace.

If God in Christ is 'reconciling all things' (see Colossians 1:20), then this is also the world we can look forward to. But can we do anything now to hasten its coming? I think we can. In 2 Corinthians 5:19, Paul says that God is 'entrusting the message of reconciliation to us'. We can, each in our own way and as a community, inspired by the Holy Spirit, play our part in reconciling the world to God and to itself, both in proclaiming the message of reconciliation and in enacting it in our daily lives.

The promise of a new creation in Christ goes way beyond 'saving' individuals for a future heaven. The message of God's incarnation which we celebrate at Christmas means that all creation is now made holy by God's presence and is worthy of our care.

In your choice of how to celebrate Christmas and the gifts you have bought, how far have you thought about the impact of your choices on the health of creation?

VERONICA ZUNDEL

God in the womb

Now the birth of Jesus the Messiah took place in this way. When his mother Mary had been engaged to Joseph, but before they lived together, she was found to be with child from the Holy Spirit… All this took place to fulfil what had been spoken by the Lord through the prophet: 'Look, the virgin shall conceive and bear a son, and they shall name him Emmanuel', which means, 'God is with us.'

'They all were looking for a king, to slay their foes and lift them high: Thou cam'st, a little baby thing, that made a woman cry.' This poem by George MacDonald (C.S. Lewis' role model as a writer) has always been a favourite of mine. The idea of God appearing on earth as a tiny, helpless child is actually quite scandalous. It is only because we have got used to it that it doesn't shock us.

'God is with us' – not a God we have to search high and low for, a God who is hidden behind a curtain of mystery, but a God who is as close as our own breath. How often do we actually live in this reality? I know it is something I find very hard to grasp. That level of intimacy with the author of all creation can be scary as well as comforting. 'Where can I go from your spirit? Or where can I flee from your presence?' asks the psalmist (Psalm 139:7). Yet it is also worth remembering that in Jesus, God chose to be emptied of all divine power and knowledge, to be a real human being in first-century Palestine, with all the limitations imposed by that. Theologians call this *kenosis*, or God's self-emptying.

We too may be called at times to empty ourselves of any power or authority we have, to be helpless in the hands of others, especially as we age. Perhaps we can be reassured by the fact that God has experienced this before us, both in the cradle and on the cross.

'My how or when Thou wilt not heed, but come down Thine own secret stair, that Thou mayst answer all my need – yea, every bygone prayer'
(George MacDonald, 1824–1905, 'That Holy Thing').

VERONICA ZUNDEL

An ordinary birth

In those days a decree went out from Emperor Augustus that all the world should be registered. This was the first registration and was taken while Quirinius was governor of Syria. All went to their own towns to be registered. Joseph also went from the town of Nazareth in Galilee to Judea, to the city of David called Bethlehem, because he was descended from the house and family of David. He went to be registered with Mary, to whom he was engaged and who was expecting a child. While they were there, the time came for her to deliver her child. And she gave birth to her firstborn son and wrapped him in bands of cloth, and laid him in a manger, because there was no place for them in the inn.

New Testament scholar R.T. France points out that the Greek word translated 'inn' in today's passage would be better rendered as 'guest chamber'. Joseph would have had relatives to stay with in Bethlehem, but with the census, the upper part of the house, where people lived, was already full with other relations. The manger would be set into the wall between the upper area and the lower area where animals were kept, and it was probably not unusual to put a baby there – as poorer people in our own culture used to put a baby in a drawer if they couldn't afford a cot.

So no inn, no innkeeper, and the ox and ass were introduced by St Francis in the 13th century. A thousand nativity plays fall apart. What remains of our 'traditional' Christmas, and does it matter? In one way, it does, because our Christmas-card versions can obscure the reality of a baby born into a normal, busy, hospitable family, but who is also about to become a refugee from forces that sought to destroy him. At the same time, our national and family Christmas traditions at their best help us to focus on the wonder of light appearing in the darkness, as portrayed by many of our greatest artists.

'Away in a manger, no crib for a bed.' How do carols and Christmas poems help you to experience the joy of Christmas?

VERONICA ZUNDEL

Unlikely messengers

In that region there were shepherds living in the fields, keeping watch over their flock by night. Then an angel of the Lord stood before them, and the glory of the Lord shone around them, and they were terrified. But the angel said to them, 'Do not be afraid; for see – I am bringing you good news of great joy for all the people: to you is born this day in the city of David a Saviour, who is the Messiah, the Lord…' So they went with haste and found Mary and Joseph, and the child lying in the manger. When they saw this, they made known what had been told them about this child; and all who heard it were amazed at what the shepherds told them. But Mary treasured all these words and pondered them in her heart.

The shepherds are another element of the Christmas story that can be over-sentimentalised. Shepherds were of low social status, regarded as dirty and unreliable, and the medieval mystery plays get it right when they include comic scenes involving this rabble. Hosts of angels appearing with an important message were certainly not part of their everyday reality. But God has always chosen unlikely messengers: the prophet Amos was a shepherd, and Balaam heard God's message through his donkey (Numbers 22:28). Shepherds, though lowly, were also used throughout the Old Testament as a way of describing the leaders of God's people, whose calling was to care for and guide them. And, of course, Jesus called himself 'the good shepherd' who lays down his life for the sheep.

Who might God choose today as an unlikely prophet? As I write this, a 16-year-old autistic Swedish girl is leading the global call to act on climate change. In my own life, it has often been through people very different from myself (including my husband) that God has taught me. Jesus encouraged us to have our ears open for God speaking at all times, and he often praised the faith of 'outsiders' – foreigners, people ostracised because of illness or disability – over the faith of his own people.

God of all, make me open to your voice,
even when it comes from unexpected places.

VERONICA ZUNDEL

Seekers and a hunter

In the time of King Herod, after Jesus was born in Bethlehem of Judea, wise men from the East came to Jerusalem, asking, 'Where is the child who has been born king of the Jews? For we observed his star at its rising, and have come to pay him homage.' When King Herod heard this, he was frightened, and all Jerusalem with him; and calling together all the chief priests and scribes of the people, he inquired of them where the Messiah was to be born. They told him, 'In Bethlehem of Judea...' Then Herod secretly called for the wise men and... sent them to Bethlehem, saying, 'Go and search diligently for the child; and when you have found him, bring me word so that I may also go and pay him homage.'

'Not everyone who says to me, "Lord, Lord," will enter the kingdom of heaven', said Jesus to his followers, 'but only one who does the will of my Father in heaven' (Matthew 7:21). Herod was a puppet king given limited autonomy by the Roman occupation, and the idea of a rival 'king of the Jews' must have indeed been a threat to him (and to those who depended on his rule). His overt desire to 'pay homage' to this royal baby masks a plot to destroy the interloper. The wise men seek Jesus, while Herod hunts him.

The wise men, although not of God's people, can read the signs of the times, and they know that something special is here. When I was a young Christian, many of my fellow Christians were suspicious of any wisdom or practice, such as meditation, that came 'from the East'. Mostly we have a more nuanced understanding now, and most people will acknowledge that God can and does speak to, and through, people from all kinds of faith tradition. We need to be 'wise as serpents' in discerning truth from lies, and 'innocent as doves' in giving respect to all people of goodwill (and even people of ill will) without judging them (see Matthew 10:16). All truth is God's truth.

'As they offered gifts most rare' (from the hymn 'As with gladness men of old'). What treasure of yours would you like to offer to God today?

VERONICA ZUNDEL

Word become flesh

In the beginning was the Word, and the Word was with God, and the Word was God. He was in the beginning with God. All things came into being through him, and without him not one thing came into being. What has come into being in him was life, and the life was the light of all people. The light shines in the darkness, and the darkness did not overcome it... He was in the world, and the world came into being through him; yet the world did not know him. He came to what was his own, and his own people did not accept him. But to all who received him, who believed in his name, he gave power to become children of God, who were born, not of blood or of the will of the flesh or of the will of man, but of God. And the Word became flesh and lived among us, and we have seen his glory, the glory as of a father's only son, full of grace and truth.

This may be the first scripture passage I ever consciously heard, as it was read in German at Coventry Cathedral every year. It is brilliant poetry, and it also contains what I, as a person of Jewish background, find the saddest verse in the Bible: 'He came unto his own, and his own received him not' (v. 11, KJV). I long for a church that can recover its Jewish roots and for a Judaism that will discover Jesus.

We need to recognise that scripture is speaking here not of itself as the word of God, but of Jesus as the Word. Before there was any written record, God was communicating with humankind in many ways: through creation, through human love, through prophecy. All these ways involved Jesus, who 'is the image of the invisible God, the firstborn of all creation; for in him all things in heaven and on earth were created... He himself is before all things, and in him all things hold together' (Colossians 1:15–17).

'Let all mortal flesh keep silence, and with fear and trembling stand...
Christ our God to earth descendeth, our full homage to demand'
(third-century hymn).

VERONICA ZUNDEL

The nativity in poetry

 Foolishly, I thought this would be an easy set of reflections to write – after all, there would be such a mass of material from which to choose! We are surrounded from the beginning of Advent by the most glorious verse; our daily lives are inhabited by carols, whether in church, at parties or even in shopping centres, creeping in between secular Christmas numbers. That, however, turned out to be the problem, as I was determined to avoid carols and instead choose poetry, which was to be read, not sung, and pondered over, rather than warbled merrily. There are fewer of these, and if we want to avoid the minefield of copyright, they are mostly Victorian and Edwardian.

It is in these eras that we see the beginning of the real weight of Christmas festivities beginning – the development of traditions, such as crackers and cards, carol-singing parties and self-indulgence, stockings packed with gifts and enormous meals. It is also in these times that the contrast between the ideal, imagined Christmas and its often-threadbare reality, both emotionally and as a luxury experience, begins to make itself felt.

But the poets are there to spot these points of irony, pinpricks of sadness and moments of doubt, and to craft them into verses that put into words the feelings we have but cannot articulate. I offer you some of the jewels I have found: verses that help us to see the poignancy of the Christmas event as well as the excitement and joy; its world-changing implications as well as its frivolous nature; and its message of hope amid times of doubt and suffering.

I hope that in the aftermath of Christmas Day, these poems will provide a useful tool for reflection at the approach of the year's end. As you look back at past events, may you see hope for the future sown into words and actions, however dark they seemed as you experienced them. As you look forward to 2021, may you find that hope growing and flourishing and be encouraged to plant more seeds, both for yourself and for others.

SALLY WELCH

On our knees

In the beginning God created the heavens and the earth… God saw all that he had made, and it was very good.

Christmas Eve, and twelve of the clock.
'Now they are all on their knees,'
An elder said as we sat in a flock
By the embers in hearthside ease…

So fair a fancy few would weave
In these years! Yet, I feel,
If someone said on Christmas Eve,
'Come; see the oxen kneel,

'In the lonely barton by yonder coomb
Our childhood used to know,'
I should go with him in the gloom,
Hoping it might be so.

('The Oxen', Thomas Hardy, 1840–1928)

Most of the nativity scenes I have known through the years involve animals around the crib. That is understandable, you will say, as the baby was born in a stable. Except, we don't know that. Since the newborn was placed 'in a manger' (Luke 2:7), our imaginations have, from earliest times, provided the stable and the animals, and they have been there ever since.

Why have the donkey, cattle and sheep remained fixed in the Christmas story? Why did the legend grow that at midnight on Christmas Eve all the animals knelt in honour of the Saviour's birth? It might be a reference to Isaiah 1:3, lamenting the lack of recognition by the Jewish people for the Messiah: 'The ox knows its owner, and the donkey its master's manger, but Israel does not know, my people do not understand.' Maybe it is nostalgia for a simpler, less questioning faith. Perhaps we should take it as a reminder that the Saviour of the world is the redeemer of all creation, and we should celebrate his birth mindful of our relationship with the natural world.

'Ox and ass before him bow… Christ is born today' (Heinrich Suso, c.1295–1366).

SALLY WELCH

Greeting with joy

The angel said to them, 'Do not be afraid. I bring you good news that will cause great joy for all the people.'

Though Darkness still her empire keep,
And hours must pass, ere morning break;
From troubled dreams, or slumbers deep,
That music kindly bids us wake:
It calls us, with an angel's voice,
To wake, and worship, and rejoice…

A sinless God, for sinful men,
Descends to suffer and to bleed;
Hell must renounce its empire then;
The price is paid, the world is freed.

('Music on Christmas Morning', Anne Brontë, 1820–49)

Despite the best efforts of those who insist there are twelve days of Christmas, most people feel that after Boxing Day it is over for the year and normalcy can return. What are we left with, apart from perhaps a feeling of exhaustion and bloat? We are left with the words of the angels: 'good news' bringing 'great joy'. Anne Brontë, whose life was not without its sorrows, is determined that we should not feel overwhelmed by darkness. Although we are far from the dawn of the kingdom, we are still called to wake, worship and rejoice. The Messiah has been born.

It is a fundamental of our faith, I believe, that the kingdom of God is in that peculiar state of being both already and not quite. We are daily surrounded by news of such appalling gravity that it is clear that 'Darkness still her empire keep'. But through the life, death and resurrection of Christ, hope for the future of the world does exist. The war, in fact, is over – death has been overthrown; truth and love will triumph. What we are witnessing are the final skirmishes, the last-ditch attempts of a failing power to maintain control over an already victorious people: 'The price is paid, the world is freed.' What greater cause for rejoicing can there be?

Lord God, help me 'to wake, and worship, and rejoice' each day.

SALLY WELCH

'For those who doubt'

A voice is heard in Ramah, weeping and great mourning, Rachel weeping for her children and refusing to be comforted, because they are no more.

While you that in your sorrow disavow
Service and hope, see love and brotherhood
Far off as ever, it will do no good
For you to wear his thorns upon your brow
For doubt of him…
Though other saviours have in older lore
A Legend, and for older gods have died –
Though death may wear the crown it always wore
And ignorance be still the sword of pride –
Something is here that was not here before,
And strangely has not yet been crucified.

('A Christmas Sonnet' by E.A. Robinson, 1869–1935)

Through the holly and the tinsel, the leftover turkey and visits to relatives, slices the cruelty of Holy Innocents Day. Desperate to see off a potential rival to his power, Herod orders the slaughter of every infant under two years old. Ironically, the holy family has already fled, so the massacre doesn't even achieve its savage purpose. Only the ordinary citizens are left, weeping and disconsolate, the joy of shepherds and angels leaving them untouched.

Many people find Christmas difficult. It may bring back memories of past misery, or present sorrow may jar with recollections of previous celebrations. This beautiful poem acknowledges that grief and the despair which can be its companion: 'you that in your sorrow disavow service and hope'. The poet does not underestimate the reader's pain, nor the self-inflicted suffering that arises when the pain gives way to doubt. He acknowledges that death may still seem to 'wear the crown it always wore', and it may appear that he too will be overcome by despair. But 'something is here that was not here before'. The world has changed because of Christ's birth. That change may be imperceptible to many, but it still exists and will do so for eternity.

Messiah, Redeemer, let me see the seeds of hope which surround me.

SALLY WELCH

Ringing out, ringing in

Now faith is the assurance of things hoped for, the conviction of things not seen.

Ring out the false, ring in the true.
Ring out the grief that saps the mind
For those that here we see no more;
Ring out the feud of rich and poor,
Ring in redress to all mankind…

Ring out the thousand wars of old,
Ring in the thousand years of peace…
Ring out the darkness of the land,
Ring in the Christ that is to be.

('In Memoriam [Ring out, wild bells]', Alfred, Lord Tennyson, 1809–92)

I am always moved by nativity plays – those simple re-enactments of the Christmas story that take place in so many schools and churches. Children share, in words and songs, the plight of the homeless family, one person's generous response and the reaction of the shepherds, people on the edge of society, to the news of the birth of the Messiah. For some children this will be the beginning of their faith story – the news that the angels bring helping them to experience the Messiah's arrival in their own hearts.

As we grow older, our faith changes, sometimes fading in the harsh light of falsehood, grief, inequality and war. We begin to question and even doubt the simple story of the stable. In some ways, it is right to do so – adult faith cannot grow properly unless its roots push deep into soil enriched by reading, listening and reflecting. Yet we must not allow our encounters with the world to destroy our hope in a better future, a time when the 'darkness of the land' is lit up by the light of Christ's love. We should try to keep a thread of childlike faith and wonder alive, shining gold with hope in the darkest times. And we should work to make this hope a certainty, helping to ring out poverty and injustice, to ring in 'the larger heart, the kindlier hand'.

'Ring out, ring out my mournful rhymes but ring the fuller minstrel in.'

SALLY WELCH

A chant sublime

In the time of King Herod, after Jesus was born in Bethlehem of Judea, wise men from the East came to Jerusalem.

I heard the bells on Christmas Day
Their old, familiar carols play…
And thought how, as the day had come,
The belfries of all Christendom
Had rolled along
The unbroken song
Of peace on earth, good-will to men!
Till ringing, singing on its way,
The world revolved from night to day,
A voice, a chime,
A chant sublime
Of peace on earth, good-will to men!

('Christmas Bells', Henry Wadsworth Longfellow, 1807–82)

When my children were young, we had a strict timetable for Christmas Day, beginning with opening stockings at 6.00 am to allow me time to take the traditional 8.00 am service. You would think that was early enough, but we would be woken up well before that time by a small child coming into our bedroom with the argument that 'somewhere in the world it's six o'clock'!

Today's poem reminds us that the birth of Christ is celebrated by Christians around the world. Just as the infant Christ received visitors 'from the East', we are drawn together as the body of Christ from every corner of the earth. Inspired by the Holy Spirit, we work to share the good news of Jesus' birth with all people – an 'unbroken song', as one after the other 'the belfries of all Christendom' announce the dawn of Christmas Day in their respective locations. Part of our task as Christians is to sing the 'song of peace on earth' in our own places, making sure this song continues unbroken as we share with each new generation, in every country, God's love for all his children.

Heavenly Father, show me how I might play a greater part in your divine chorus – the 'chant sublime' that announces peace on earth.

SALLY WELCH

The holy star

'Go therefore and make disciples of all nations, baptising them in the name of the Father and of the Son and of the Holy Spirit.'

As shadows cast by cloud and sun,
Flit o'er the summer grass,
So, in thy sight, Almighty One!
Earth's generations pass…

Yet doth the star of Bethlehem shed
A lustre pure and sweet;
And still it leads, as once it led,
To the Messiah's feet.

O Father, may that holy star
Grow every year more bright,
And send its glorious beams afar
To fill the world with light.

('The Star of Bethlehem', William Cullen Bryant, 1794–1878)

There is a strong sense in this poem of the limited span of years we have on this earth. As briefly as summer shadows, we arrive, live out our time and then are gathered once more to the Father. The sense of time passing may find an echo in our hearts at this end of the year, as we pause to reflect on the past twelve months. The opportunity awaits us to mourn and perhaps fear our approaching end, but the poet does not leave us without hope. He reminds us that the 'star of Bethlehem' still shines brightly, guiding all who look to it for help to the source of the one true light. But there is a sense also in the final verse that we can be part of that guidance. Just as a mirror reflects beams of light even further into the darkness, so we can reflect the light of the star ever more widely into our community and beyond, sharing hope and love in our everyday encounters, 'to fill the world with light'.

Heavenly Father, as we look to the challenges and delights of 2021,
give us the grace to share in your glorious light and reflect that light
in our words and actions.

SALLY WELCH

Reading *New Daylight* in a group

SALLY WELCH

I am aware that although some of you cherish the moments of quiet during the day which enable you to read and reflect on the passages we offer you in *New Daylight*, other readers prefer to study in small groups, to enable conversation and discussion and the sharing of insights. With this in mind, here are some ideas for discussion starters within a study group. Some of the questions are generic and can be applied to any set of contributions within this issue; others are specific to certain sets of readings. I hope they generate some interesting reflections and conversations!

General discussion starters

These can be used for any study series within this issue. Remember there are no right or wrong answers – these questions are simply to enable a group to engage in conversation.

- What do you think the main idea or theme of the author in this series? Do you think they succeeded in communicating this to you, or were you more interested in the side issues?

- Have you had any experience of the issues that are raised in the study? How have they affected your life?

- What evidence does the author use to support their ideas? Do they use personal observations and experience, facts, quotations from other authorities? Which appeals to you most?

- Does the author make a 'call to action'? Is that call realistic and achievable? Do you think their ideas will work in the secular world?

- Can you identify specific passages that struck you personally – as interesting, profound, difficult to understand or illuminating?

- Did you learn something new reading this series? Will you think differently about some things, and if so, what are they?

Questions for specific series

A Celtic Advent – David Cole

David prefers to use the word 'Divine' instead of the traditional 'God'. Do you find this helpful? What is your image of God? How much is it shaped by your own experience? In what other ways might God be depicted?

Home – Tony Horsfall

Tony writes: 'Religious homes, rightly or wrongly, are often portrayed in books and films as being strict and joyless, with little room for personal freedom' (14 October). Do you agree with this? How might people entering your home know your faith? Do our homes really reflect our personality?

Tony shows the importance of offering and accepting hospitality – how might our homes be made more hospitable?

Our creator God – Ruth Bancewicz et al.

In her introduction, Ruth writes of the importance of an 'informed perspective'. How have the scientists helped you to see creation differently?

Wilson Poon writes: 'Biblical wisdom is about alignment with God's creational intent' (5 September). How aligned are we today with God's intention for creation? In what ways can we draw closer to God's original design for creation?

Meet the author: Amanda Bloor

Amanda, you have had a varied ministry – Cadet Forces' chaplain, bishops' chaplain, assistant diocesan director for ordinands and now vicar on the Isle of Wight. Do you see a pattern in this?

When God called me to ministry, I thought that it was a ridiculous idea and that I must have misheard. But as I began to accept the vocation and go through the discernment process, the varied strands of my life up to that point began to be drawn together in quite an unexpected way. Priesthood has continued that process. Every new experience builds on the past and helps me to grow in faith and confidence that with God's help all things are possible. As for the years ahead – well, that's in God's hands!

You have been a vocal advocate of women's ministry – how did this come about? Has the 'battle' now been won?

I don't think I'd call it a battle, but a process of education. I'm proud to call myself a feminist, because I believe that when Jesus talked about abundant life for all, he included women! I'm grateful to the Christian men and women who thought, prayed and campaigned to make the ordination of women possible. I hope that we can use that process to begin to address the concerns of other groups who feel marginalised or excluded by the church. We're all made in God's image and we all matter.

You write in this issue on 'praying with objects' – what is your preferred method of prayer?

I found my spiritual home in the Church of England partly because of the liturgy. I love the fact that there's a framework that holds us together, and written prayers are great on days when I'm tired or feeling uninspired. I send up quick arrow prayers, too, and I find long walks help me to connect with God. Music can also inspire prayer.

How do you relax?

I walk, I go for a run, I cook, I read and I play in our village band – making music with others is wonderful. I'm lucky enough to live by the sea, so a long walk on the beach is a real stress-buster.

Recommended reading

Following on from the success of *At Home in Lent*, Gordon Giles takes a journey through Advent to Christmas and beyond in the company of familiar seasonal and domestic objects and experiences.

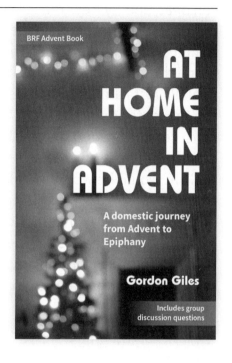

Focusing on the everyday stuff we typically associate with this time of year, including some things not so festive, he reflects on their spiritual significance, meaning and message in today's world. Beginning with chapters on journeying and travel, the book moves though major Advent themes of expectation, waiting, mortality and hope to the joy of incarnation and salvation.

The following extract is from the reflection for 20 December, entitled 'Christmas carols: missionary music'.

As God's chosen ones, holy and beloved, clothe yourselves with compassion, kindness, humility, meekness, and patience. Bear with one another and, if anyone has a complaint against another, forgive each other; just as the Lord has forgiven you, so you also must forgive. Above all, clothe yourselves with love, which binds everything together in perfect harmony. And let the peace of Christ rule in your hearts, to which indeed you were called in the one body. And be thankful. Let the word of Christ dwell in you richly; teach and admonish one another in all wisdom; and with gratitude in your hearts sing psalms, hymns, and spiritual songs to God. And whatever you do, in word or deed, do everything in the name of the Lord Jesus, giving thanks to God the Father through him.

COLOSSIANS 3:12–17 (NRSV)

At this time of year there is a very perceptible crescendo of carol singing as we approach Christmas Day. Radio stations have their sonic equivalent of the Advent calendar, increasing the Christmas flavour as the anticipation mounts, so much so that by Christmas Eve Classic FM plays little else. Strictly speaking the Christmas season begins on Christmas Eve (not 1 December), by which time many people have heard as many Christmas carols as they can bear, and by New Year's Day the Christmas music has diminished and normal service is resumed. The popular song 'The Twelve Days of Christmas' reminds us that there are twelve days after Christmas in the season, and we might remember that Christmastide evolves into Epiphanytide, which actually lasts until Candlemas on 2 February, when the church celebrates the Presentation of Christ in the Temple. The Christmas season lasts 40 days. Yet if we added that to the run-up to Christmas, we would have two months of Christmas carols!

That would be wonderful. Most Christmas carols are actually hymns of praise to God, extolling the virtues of divine love, the saving work of God and the theology of incarnation and reminding us of the biblical story. At no other time of the year do we hear so much Christian gospel in our shops, on our streets and on the airwaves. For some people, carol singing is the sound of Christmas and even if they never darken the doors of a church, they love carols.

Many people do come to church at Christmas. Church of England statistics reveal that around 2.5 million people have attended carol services consistently over the past decade. Nine Lessons and Carols services have been held for a century now and still attract large numbers, especially if candlelit. The service provides a staple menu of Christmas hymns sung by the congregation, carols sung by a choir and readings from the Bible that tell of the 'run-up to Christmas', and it culminates with some hard-core theology, found in the final reading of John 1. Likewise the related *Carols from Kings* television broadcast, while not the same content as the service, attracts millions of viewers on Christmas Eve afternoon, especially for the music. These broadcasts and services in cathedrals and churches epitomise Christmas for many people.

Many Christmas carols are macaronic (sung in two languages), especially those which quote the angels' '*gloria*' in Latin. When church services were in Latin, the people generally did not understand much of what was said or sung, but the '*gloria*' was familiar. The tradition has remained, and '*gloria in excelsis*' is a frequent refrain in carols, such as 'Angels from the Realms of Glory', 'Ding Dong Merrily on High' and the Basque carol 'The Angel Gabriel'.

Nowadays there is still a need to sing every carol in two languages: not Latin and English, but the languages of faith and of fun. When we sing 'While Shepherds Watched Their Flocks by Night' or 'Hark the Herald Angels Sing', we may or may not be affirming the message of the lyrics. Take 'While Shepherds Watched'. Arguably the first English hymn ever written, it originally appeared in the supplement to *A New Version of the Psalms of David* in 1700. In some editions it was entitled 'Song of the Angels at the Nativity of our Blessed Saviour'. Based on the angels' song from Luke 2:14, it is not a psalm, which is why it appeared in the supplement, allowed in as a scriptural paraphrase. The point is, a hymn such as this, which expounds and reflects upon the story of Christmas, is sung in pubs and schools by all and sundry, only some of whom are aware of, or believe in, what they are singing. Likewise with 'Hark the Herald Angels Sing': atheists and those of other faiths join in singing of the one who was 'born that man no more may die, born to raise the sons of earth, born to give them second birth'. Similarly, Christina Rossetti's 'In the Bleak Midwinter', set to music so beautifully by Gustav Holst, Harold Darke and more recently Bob Chilcott, concludes with the profound verse:

> What can I give him,
> poor as I am?
> If I were a shepherd,
> I would bring a lamb.
> If I were a wise man,
> I would do my part.
> Yet what I can I give him,
> give my heart.

One might reflect on what is going on internally for those who sing this carol but who do not mean anything by it. Others love singing carols, and they mean what they sing; such carol singing is macaronic in a modern sense: festive and faithful. Obviously, and delightfully, it is possible and desirable to be both. In doing so, and in being both, our hope and prayer is everyone might come to believe what they sing and sing what they believe.

There are trivial carols and modern Christmas songs, some sillier than others. Yet even some of the Christmas classics have something to say to us, even if they make no mention of the nativity or incarnation. 'White Christmas' is a wonderful song, and there is no harm singing it (even if it is set in summertime). Songs about Santa are fun and flippant and stand in the Dickensian tradition of being kind, being with family and having fun. Many Christmas 'weepy' movies play this card too. Greg Lake, who wrote

'I Believe in Father Christmas' in 1974, has been accused of writing an anti-Christian song, yet it seems he wrote it as a protest against the commercialisation of Christmas and an affirmation of family warmth and forgiveness. What seems antithetical to the season might not be. Contrast this with 'It Came Upon the Midnight Clear', which was written by Edmund Sears, a unitarian who did not believe in the Christian Trinity. The carol does not mention Jesus at all, yet it is often sung at midnight services because it has the word 'midnight' in its first line and mentions Christmas themes, such as angels and peace on earth. 'Away in a Manger' is a hugely popular cradle carol, but its lyrics do not bear serious theological scrutiny.

Christmas carols can be complex. Yet carol singing is a wonderful, fun, unifying, reflective thing to do at this time of year. Long may it continue, and long may the angels' song and the story of salvation through incarnation resound in our churches, pubs, streets and concert halls.

Reflection

Do you think about what you sing? As you sing carols, reflect on what they are really saying to you and others.

Next time you sing or hear a carol, pay attention to the lyrics: are they true? Pray for all church musicians at this time of year, and give thanks for the gift of music.

Prayer (based on the Choristers' Prayer)

O Lord, grant that what we sing with our lips, we may believe in our hearts, and what we believe in our hearts, we may show forth in our lives. Amen

To order a copy of this book, please use the order form on page 149 or visit **brfonline.org.uk**.

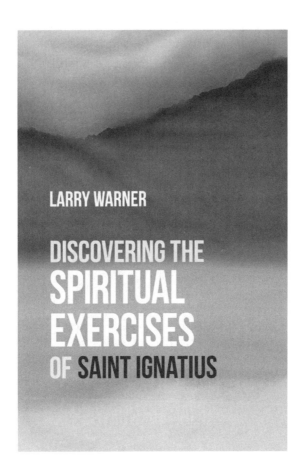

For nearly 500 years, the Exercises have been a tool for spiritual formation. Their popularity has ebbed and flowed, but they are now experiencing something of a revival across the breadth of the church. This is not a book about the methods or techniques of Christian formation; rather it is a book that enables you to come before God through the gospel narratives in order to encounter Jesus afresh. If you hunger for something deeper and yearn to walk with Jesus (not just read about him), this book is for you.

Discovering the Spiritual Exercises of Saint Ignatius
Larry Warner
978 0 85746 977 9 £12.99
brfonline.org.uk

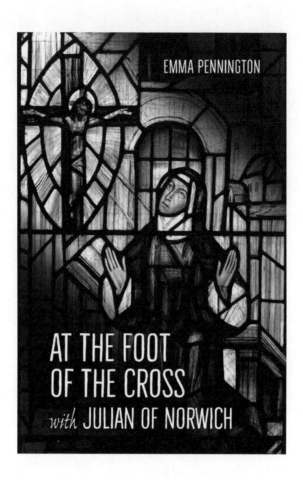

'All shall be well, and all shall be well, and all manner of thing shall be well.' This quotation is all that many people know of the 14th-century anchoress Julian of Norwich. This book seeks to redress that, bringing the reader into a devotional engagement with Julian's other meditations. Each chapter centres on one aspect or image from Julian's Revelation to provide a meditation that enables the reader to linger on the wonder of the cross, ending with a prayer that leads to silence and a thought or verse to carry into daily life.

At the Foot of the Cross with Julian of Norwich
Emma Pennington
978 0 85746 519 1 £8.99
brfonline.org.uk

To order

Online: **brfonline.org.uk**
Telephone: +44 (0)1865 319700
Mon–Fri 9.15–17.30

Delivery times within the UK are normally 15 working days. Prices are correct at the time of going to press but may change without prior notice.

Title	Price	Qty	Total
BRF Advent Book: At Home in Advent	£8.99		
Discovering the Spiritual Exercises of Saint Ignatius	£12.99		
At the Foot of the Cross with Julian of Norwich	£8.99		

POSTAGE AND PACKING CHARGES			
Order value	UK	Europe	Rest of world
Under £7.00	£2.00		
£7.00–£29.99	£3.00	Available on request	Available on request
£30.00 and over	FREE		

Total value of books	
Postage and packing	
Total for this order	

Please complete in BLOCK CAPITALS

Title _____ First name/initials _____ Surname _____

Address _____

_____ Postcode _____

Acc. No. _____ Telephone _____

Email _____

Method of payment

☐ Cheque (made payable to BRF) ☐ MasterCard / Visa

Card no. [ ][ ][ ][ ] [ ][ ][ ][ ] [ ][ ][ ][ ] [ ][ ][ ][ ]

Expires end [ ][ ] [ ][ ]   Security code* [ ][ ][ ]   Last 3 digits on the reverse of the card

Signature* _____ Date _____ / _____ / _____
*ESSENTIAL IN ORDER TO PROCESS YOUR ORDER

Please return this form to:

BRF, 15 The Chambers, Vineyard, Abingdon OX14 3FE | **enquiries@brf.org.uk**
To read our terms and find out about cancelling your order, please visit **brfonline.org.uk/terms**.

The Bible Reading Fellowship (BRF) is a Registered Charity (233280)

BRF needs you!

If you're one of our many thousands of regular *New Daylight* readers, you will know all about the rich rewards of regular Bible reading and the value of daily notes to guide, inform and inspire you.

Here are some recent comments from *New Daylight* readers:

'Thank you for all the many inspiring writings that help so much when things are tough.'

'Just right for me – I learned a lot!'

'We looked forward to each day's message as we pondered each passage and comment.'

If you have similarly positive things to say about *New Daylight*, would you be willing to share your experience with others? Could you follow the example of long-standing *New Daylight* reader Beryl Fudge and form a *New Daylight* reading group, not to take the place of private prayer and reading but to share insights and deepen understanding? 'I've quite a few friends who also take the notes and we discuss them in the group,' says Beryl. 'There's so much in them every day. What I most value in *New Daylight* is the way they connect the Old and New Testament scriptures with what's happening here and now.'

It doesn't need to be complicated: every issue of *New Daylight* includes questions for reflection or discussion.

We can supply further information if you need it and would love to hear about it if you do form a *New Daylight* reading group.

For more information:

- Email **enquiries@brf.org.uk**
- Telephone BRF on +44 (0)1865 319700 Mon–Fri 9.15–17.30
- Write to us at BRF, 15 The Chambers, Vineyard, Abingdon OX14 3FE

Enabling all ages to grow in faith

At BRF, we long for people of all ages to grow in faith and understanding of the Bible. That's what all our work as a charity is about.

- Our **Living Faith** range of resources helps Christians go deeper in their understanding of scripture, in prayer and in their walk with God. Our conferences and events bring people together to share this journey.

- We also want to make it easier for local churches to engage effectively in ministry and mission – by helping them bring new families into a growing relationship with God through **Messy Church** or by supporting churches as they nurture the spiritual life of older people through **Anna Chaplaincy**.

- Our **Holy Habits** resources help whole congregations grow together as disciples of Jesus, living out and sharing their faith.

- Our **Parenting for Faith** team coaches parents and others to raise God-connected children and teens, and enables churches to fully support them.

- We also offer a professional education service, **Barnabas in Schools**, giving primary schools confidence, expertise and opportunities for exploring Christianity in creative ways that engage all pupils.

Do you share our vision?

Though a significant proportion of BRF's funding is generated through our charitable activities, we are dependent on the generous support of individuals, churches and charitable trusts.

If you share our vision, would you help us to enable even more people of all ages to grow in faith? Your prayers and financial support are vital for the work that we do. You could:

- Support BRF's ministry with a regular donation;
- Support us with a one-off gift;
- Consider leaving a gift to BRF in your will (see page 152);
- Encourage your church to support BRF as part of your church's giving to home mission – perhaps focusing on a specific ministry or programme;
- Most important of all, support BRF with your prayers.

Donate at **brf.org.uk/donate** or use the form on pages 153–54.

Building a legacy: each person plays their part

Eliashib the high priest and his fellow priests went to work and rebuilt the Sheep Gate. They dedicated it and set its doors in place, building as far as the Tower of the Hundred, which they dedicated, and as far as the Tower of Hananel. The men of Jericho built the adjoining section, and Zakkur son of Imri built next to them.

NEHEMIAH 3:1–2 (NIV)

Nehemiah 3 recounts the story of the rebuilding of the walls of Jerusalem. A host of names follow in quick succession. While it's perhaps not the Bible passage I would like to be asked to read aloud at the front of church for fear of mispronunciation, this chapter is one of my firm favourites from the whole of the Bible and one that I return to frequently.

The Bible affirms that each person is important, made in the image of God, and that each person in the church has a part to play. The different parts come together to make the whole, and they cannot function without each other.

I know of many who at times have felt overstretched or underappreciated in their work and ministry, perhaps feeling that no one notices. Nehemiah 3 reminds us that every stone laid, every timber cut and every work undertaken is seen by God, and he knows his workers by name.

Throughout BRF's story, our ministry has grown beyond our expectation, thanks to those who have given generously, prayed faithfully and served tirelessly without seeking recognition.

They – and you – are known by God. Thank you. Could you help support this work?

> Give – Pray – Get involved

If you would like some information about leaving a gift in your will to BRF, please get in touch with us at **+44 (0)1235 462305** or **giving@brf.org.uk**.

> **brf.org.uk/lastingdifference**

I would like to make a gift to support BRF. Please use my gift for:

☐ Where it is most needed ☐ Anna Chaplaincy ☐ Barnabas in Schools
☐ Messy Church ☐ Parenting for Faith

Title	First name/initials	Surname

Address

Postcode

Email

Telephone

Signature	Date

giftaid it You can add an extra 25p to every £1 you give.

Please treat as Gift Aid donations all qualifying gifts of money made

☐ today, ☐ in the past four years, ☐ and in the future.

I am a UK taxpayer and understand that if I pay less Income Tax and/or Capital Gains Tax in the current tax year than the amount of Gift Aid claimed on all my donations, it is my responsibility to pay any difference.

☐ My donation does not qualify for Gift Aid.

Please notify BRF if you want to cancel this Gift Aid declaration, change your name or home address, or no longer pay sufficient tax on your income and/or capital gains.

We will use your personal data to process this transaction. From time to time we may send information about the work of BRF that we think may be of interest to you. Our privacy policy is at **brf.org.uk/privacy**. Please contact us if you wish to discuss your mailing preferences.

Please complete other side of form ➜

SHARING OUR VISION – MAKING A GIFT

Regular giving

By Direct Debit: You can set up a Direct Debit quickly and easily at **brf.org.uk/donate**

By Standing Order: Please contact our Fundraising Administrator +44 (0)1865 319700 | **giving@brf.org.uk**

One-off donation

Please accept my gift of:

☐ £10 ☐ £50 ☐ £100 Other £ [   ]

by (*delete as appropriate*):

☐ Cheque/Charity Voucher payable to 'BRF'

☐ MasterCard/Visa/Debit card/Charity card

Name on card

Card no. [ ][ ][ ][ ] [ ][ ][ ][ ] [ ][ ][ ][ ] [ ][ ][ ][ ]

Expires end [M][M] [Y][Y] Security code* [ ][ ][ ]

*Last 3 digits on the reverse of the card
ESSENTIAL IN ORDER TO PROCESS
YOUR PAYMENT

Signature   Date

☐ I would like to leave a gift to BRF in my will. Please send me further information.

For help or advice regarding making a gift, please contact our Fundraising Administrator +44 (0)1865 319700

Registered with

FUNDRAISING **REGULATOR**

↩ Please complete other side of form

Please return this form to:
BRF, 15 The Chambers, Vineyard, Abingdon OX14 3FE

The Bible Reading Fellowship is a Registered Charity (233280)

ND0320

NEW DAYLIGHT SUBSCRIPTION RATES

Please note our new subscription rates, current until 30 April 2021:

Individual subscriptions
covering 3 issues for under 5 copies, payable in advance
(including postage & packing):

	UK	Europe	Rest of world
New Daylight	£17.85	£25.80	£29.70
New Daylight 3-year subscription (9 issues) (not available for Deluxe)	£50.85	N/A	N/A
New Daylight Deluxe per set of 3 issues p.a.	£22.35	£32.55	£38.55

Group subscriptions
covering 3 issues for 5 copies or more, sent to one UK address (post free):

New Daylight	£14.10 per set of 3 issues p.a.
New Daylight Deluxe	£17.85 per set of 3 issues p.a.

Overseas group subscription rates
Available on request. Please email **enquiries@brf.org.uk**.

Copies may also be obtained from Christian bookshops:

New Daylight	£4.70 per copy
New Daylight Deluxe	£5.95 per copy

All our Bible reading notes can be ordered online by visiting
brfonline.org.uk/collections/subscriptions

New Daylight
New Daylight is also available as an app for Android, iPhone and iPad
brfonline.org.uk/collections/apps

NEW DAYLIGHT INDIVIDUAL SUBSCRIPTION FORM

> All our Bible reading notes can be ordered online by visiting
> **brfonline.org.uk/collections/subscriptions**

☐ I would like to take out a subscription:

Title _____ First name/initials _____ Surname _____

Address _____

_____ Postcode _____

Telephone _____ Email _____

Please send *New Daylight* beginning with the January 2021 / May 2021 / September 2021 issue (*delete as appropriate*):

(*please tick box*)	UK	Europe	Rest of world
New Daylight 1-year subscription	☐ £17.85	☐ £25.80	☐ £29.70
New Daylight 3-year subscription	☐ £50.85	N/A	N/A
New Daylight Deluxe	☐ £22.35	☐ £32.55	☐ £38.55

Total enclosed £ _____ (cheques should be made payable to 'BRF')

Please charge my MasterCard / Visa ☐ Debit card ☐ with £ _____

Card no. ☐☐☐☐ ☐☐☐☐ ☐☐☐☐ ☐☐☐☐

Expires end ☐☐ ☐☐ Security code* ☐☐☐   Last 3 digits on the reverse of the card

Signature* _____ Date _____/_____/_____

*ESSENTIAL IN ORDER TO PROCESS YOUR PAYMENT

To set up a Direct Debit, please also complete the Direct Debit instruction on page 159 and return it to BRF with this form.

Please return this form with the appropriate payment to:
BRF, 15 The Chambers, Vineyard, Abingdon OX14 3FE

To read our terms and find out about cancelling your order, please visit **brfonline.org.uk/terms**.

The Bible Reading Fellowship is a Registered Charity (233280)

ND0320

NEW DAYLIGHT GIFT SUBSCRIPTION FORM

☐ I would like to give a gift subscription (please provide both names and addresses):

Title _____ First name/initials _____ Surname _____

Address _____

_____ Postcode _____

Telephone _____ Email _____

Gift subscription name _____

Gift subscription address _____

_____ Postcode _____

Gift message (20 words max. or include your own gift card):

_____

_____

Please send *New Daylight* beginning with the January 2021 / May 2021 / September 2021 issue (*delete as appropriate*):

(*please tick box*)	UK	Europe	Rest of world
New Daylight 1-year subscription	☐ £17.85	☐ £25.80	☐ £29.70
New Daylight 3-year subscription	☐ £50.85	N/A	N/A
New Daylight Deluxe	☐ £22.35	☐ £32.55	☐ £38.55

Total enclosed £ _____ (cheques should be made payable to 'BRF')

Please charge my MasterCard / Visa ☐ Debit card ☐ with £ _____

Card no. ☐☐☐☐ ☐☐☐☐ ☐☐☐☐ ☐☐☐☐

Expires end ☐☐ ☐☐   Security code* ☐☐☐   Last 3 digits on the reverse of the card

Signature* _____ Date _____/_____/_____

*ESSENTIAL IN ORDER TO PROCESS YOUR PAYMENT

To set up a Direct Debit, please also complete the Direct Debit instruction on page 159 and return it to BRF with this form.

Please return this form with the appropriate payment to:
BRF, 15 The Chambers, Vineyard, Abingdon OX14 3FE

To read our terms and find out about cancelling your order, please visit **brfonline.org.uk/terms**.

The Bible Reading Fellowship is a Registered Charity (233280)

You can pay for your annual subscription to our Bible reading notes using Direct Debit. You need only give your bank details once, and the payment is made automatically every year until you cancel it. If you would like to pay by Direct Debit, please use the form opposite, entering your BRF account number under 'Reference number'.

You are fully covered by the Direct Debit Guarantee:

The Direct Debit Guarantee

- This Guarantee is offered by all banks and building societies that accept instructions to pay Direct Debits.

- If there are any changes to the amount, date or frequency of your Direct Debit, The Bible Reading Fellowship will notify you 10 working days in advance of your account being debited or as otherwise agreed. If you request The Bible Reading Fellowship to collect a payment, confirmation of the amount and date will be given to you at the time of the request.

- If an error is made in the payment of your Direct Debit, by The Bible Reading Fellowship or your bank or building society, you are entitled to a full and immediate refund of the amount paid from your bank or building society.

- If you receive a refund you are not entitled to, you must pay it back when The Bible Reading Fellowship asks you to.

- You can cancel a Direct Debit at any time by simply contacting your bank or building society. Written confirmation may be required. Please also notify us.

The Bible Reading Fellowship

Instruction to your bank or building society to pay by Direct Debit

Please fill in the whole form using a ballpoint pen and return it to:
BRF, 15 The Chambers, Vineyard, Abingdon OX14 3FE

Service User Number: | 5 | 5 | 8 | 2 | 2 | 9 |

Name and full postal address of your bank or building society

To: The Manager	Bank/Building Society
Address	
	Postcode

Name(s) of account holder(s)

Branch sort code

| | | – | | | – | | |

Bank/Building Society account number

| | | | | | | | | |

Reference number

| | | | | | | | |

Instruction to your Bank/Building Society
Please pay The Bible Reading Fellowship Direct Debits from the account detailed in this instruction, subject to the safeguards assured by the Direct Debit Guarantee. I understand that this instruction may remain with The Bible Reading Fellowship and, if so, details will be passed electronically to my bank/building society.

Signature(s)

Banks and Building Societies may not accept Direct Debit instructions for some types of account.

Enabling all ages to grow in faith

Anna Chaplaincy

Barnabas in Schools

Holy Habits

Living Faith

Messy Church

Parenting for Faith

The Bible Reading Fellowship (BRF) is a Christian charity that resources individuals and churches and provides a professional education service to primary schools.

Our vision is to enable people of all ages to grow in faith and understanding of the Bible and to see more people equipped to exercise their gifts in leadership and ministry.

To find out more about our ministries and programmes, visit

brf.org.uk